NICHOLAS KALASHNIKOFF

Jumper

London
OXFORD UNIVERSITY PRESS
1972

Oxford University Press, Ely House, London W. 1
GLASGOW NEW YORK TORONTO MELBOURNE WELLINGTON
CAPE TOWN IBADAN NAIROBI DAR ES SALAAM LUSAKA ADDIS ABABA
DELHI BOMBAY CALCUTTA MADRAS KARACHI LAHORE DACCA
KUALA LUMPUR SINGAPORE HONG KONG TOKYO

First published in the United States of America
by Charles Scribner's Sons, New York

First published in the U.K. 1963
Reprinted 1970
First published in this edition 1972

ISBN 0 19 272032 5

Printed in Holland
Zuid-Nederlandsche Drukkerij N.V.
's-Hertogenbosch

Author's Note

Jumper was a Siberian horse and my friend. He was gentle, wise, courageous, loyal and understanding to a rare degree. It is seldom that one can say more than that of anyone, whether man or beast. Fate happily brought us together in the defence of our country, when for a time our destinies were strangely linked. He was already a seasoned campaigner, having served several masters with the same devotion he was to give me. In return he asked nothing save care and a measure of affection. These I gave him wholeheartedly for I valued him as I would a person near and dear. In writing his story, out of my own memories and as I got it from the lips of others who loved him, I pay a debt of gratitude not to Jumper alone but to countless horses who have unwittingly and uncomplainingly shared in the tragedies men create.

PART I

Chapter 1

In the soft light of the northern winter night earth and sky lay wrapped in peace. The stars looked down from distant heights upon white-clad hills, forests, plains, and the immense expanse that was Lake Baikal, frozen over now and breathlessly quiet. Sparks from the chimneys made fantastic patterns against the heavens, then died in the mist. It was a fairy-like picture, with the houses of the village of Kabansk standing out like black dominoes against nature's snowy screen.

Occasionally the anguished howls of wolves ravenous for food broke the stillness. In reply, dogs barked in excited chorus, giving notice to the marauders that they were at their posts and not to be caught napping. There was no other sound.

Except for the sparks from chimneys, the houses were dark, and even the chimneys were becoming less animated minute by minute. Siberians do not believe in wasting firewood. If at any time during the night a fire is kept actively alive you may be sure it is not a whim, but some urgent need.

Signs indicated that everyone in the village was asleep, except those in the household of Gerasim Ozerov. Sparks pouring skyward singled out the house, lying prominently in the very centre of the village.

It was Gerasim himself, a robust peasant with a bushy, greying beard, who threw fresh logs onto the fire and waited. He had no thought of sleep. He was greatly worried. Nine days ago, by careful reckoning, the old black mare, his favourite, was due to foal. Nine days, and still not a sign. This was bad, especially so because she refused food and obviously was suffering. Every time he approached her she breathed heavily, like a human being in pain, and yet there was nothing he could do. The bitter weather added complications. Although the stable floor was covered with straw and all cracks were stuffed against the searching wind, there was danger that the colt would freeze should he miss the foaling. This was the thing he dreaded. This was the reason he, or some-one of the household, stayed awake all night.

Beside Gerasim, near the fire, a boy sat reading in a droning voice from a large book on the care of horses. The boy was Gerasim's son, Denis, ten years old and lame. Even when he was sitting, one could see that one of his legs was different from the other.

Gerasim listened, half-dozing. After a time he roused himself and, picking up the lantern, left the warmth of the fire to visit the stall where the mare stood, her head drooping, her belly incredibly distended. With one hand stroking the animal's broad quarters he shook his head and plucked at his beard. 'Be patient, Dowager,' he said soothingly. 'It won't be much longer, if God lets everything go well. Try to drop the colt. Whatever is ailing you? This is not your first. You've given me many fine colts. Now be a good girl and gladden our hearts again.'

The animal's suffering gave Gerasim an odd feeling of helpless-ness, for in his village he was considered an authority in all matters relating to cattle and horses, a first-rate veterinarian—self-taught. The peasants always sought his help in a difficult case and he never refused. For his services he accepted trifling gifts or vodka but no money. He was very obstinate about this, being content with the esteem of his neighbours. It was cause for rejoicing when one of his patients got well, and cause for grief when one died. Then he bewailed his ignorance, which denied him the skill of trained veterinarians who, according to rumour, performed miracles by operating on animals as doctors do on human beings.

He looked at the mare and called to mind other instances of difficult foaling in his experience. Yes, all was not well. Delay in foaling was not in itself unusual. A mare couldn't be expected to drop her burden precisely on the minute. But nine days, and such an old mare as Dowager. . . . That was cause for concern.

Before he left the stable he examined the mare, wiped her watering eyes, and crept under her and placed his ear to her belly, trying to detect signs of another life. Was there a movement? Or was the sound only a rumbling in the intestines, as it had been so many times before?

Feeling only slightly reassured, Gerasim returned to the house. The boy, who was on the verge of falling asleep, roused himself, picked up the book and went on reading where he had left off. *The Horse and How to Care for It* was the title of the volume. Gerasim had inherited it from his father and knew most of it by heart.

Sitting there listening to the boy's droning voice, dark thoughts assailed him. Here was Denis, born with a deformed foot, a perpetual reminder of someone's carelessness. With peasant logic he thought: If my woman bore many children successfully, and yet injured the last child in her belly, then a like evil can befall the mare. Maybe she hit herself against something. Perhaps she fell. How can you tell? Maybe the colt is dead inside her.

Gerasim hated to think of it, because this time he had mated Dowager with a rare, visiting stallion, and he looked forward with more than ordinary interest to the offspring of that union.

It had happened like this. The stallion was on his way to be delivered to the owner of a nearby gold mine when he suddenly developed a lameness in one leg. An odd-looking creature, he resembled a big hare rather than a horse. The man in charge of him brought him to Gerasim. 'Help me, Gerasim,' he begged. 'I'll lose my job if I bring the master a lame beast. This is no ordinary horse. He has English blood and won a prize at the races in Tomsk. If you will cure him I'll pay you out of my own pocket.'

Gerasim examined the animal thoroughly but could find nothing seriously wrong. One front leg was slightly swollen near the knee—the result of a slight knock or a misstep—but the bones were uninjured. After several days of poulticing with hay and bran the swelling went down. The keeper was delighted and wanted to pay Gerasim there and then, but Gerasim refused. Instead he asked permission to mate the stallion with his finest mare.

'All right,' the man agreed. 'But why? What do you want with this mongrel? He's useless for farming. What will you do with a horse of his breed? Parade around with him? You need an animal that is strong, one that can plough and drive across the taiga in any weather. Beasts like this are for rich people to use for sport or show. Those who have more money than they know what to do with can spend it on such playthings. What is there to him? Neither beauty nor strength.'

Gerasim scratched the back of his head as he answered good-naturedly: 'I don't agree with you, my friend. I have a feeling that if we mate his elegance with my Dowager we might produce an excellent breed. I have read about such things in books, also some clever people have told me. Anyway, we'll try.'

The man shook his head but said no more.

The mating went off well, and Gerasim himself attended the mare during the next eleven months. Never before had he given a horse such attention.

Now, thinking of all these things, he interrupted the boy, and said dolefully: 'We are ignorant people, Denis. We don't know anything. Maybe we shouldn't have crossed the mare with the English mongrel. But it was such a temptation. Think! If Dowager will give birth to a stallion, and we rear him, he will provide for the whole village. What a breed that will be—Siberian-English! It strikes me that it should be a mighty fine horse.'

Denis answered quickly and with enthusiasm, imitating his father's voice:

'Of course. It will be splendid to have a stallion. Improve the breed here, too.'

It meant a great deal to the boy to be allowed to discuss such an important household matter, and to a peasant nothing is more important than the increase of his livestock. It meant that Gerasim valued his, Denis's, opinion, as he would that of an adult. It confirmed the promise his father had made him only two days ago before the icon, when he had said, crossing himself: 'Let God be gracious and help Dowager drop her colt. That colt will be yours. On my word of honour.'

To have a horse of his very own! Since that moment Denis had been beside himself. His father's anxiety was his anxiety. There was nothing he would not do to help. When his father slept he stayed awake to keep an eye on the mare, and through the day on the slightest pretext he would grab his hat and jacket and pay a visit to the stable. His mother was provoked with both of them. 'The old man and the youngster have lost their minds,' she grumbled, 'and we'll all die of the cold if they don't stop opening the door every other minute.'

Feeling the responsibility of ownership, Denis also worried about the mare, but his thoughts were not Gerasim's thoughts. He knew something of the business of bringing life into the world —what peasant boy doesn't? It was fascinating and mysterious to think that Dowager's grotesque body, which she supported with difficulty by planting her feet wide apart, held a fully formed colt! A miracle! It was only necessary for her to let go of it, and he believed it would help if she could scream. He remembered when the wife of his eldest brother had had her child, how she had shrieked and how the midwife had soothed her, saying, 'That's right, my dear. Cry out as loud as you can and push hard and you won't even notice when the baby comes.'

Was it really so? At any rate the woman gave birth to a lusty girl. He thought sagely, 'That's what Dowager should do—scream. It would be easier for her.'

But her mare was silent. She just stood for hours at a time, not daring to lie down, because once her legs gave way under the burden she was afraid she would not rise again. Now and then she moved laboriously from one corner of the stall to another, and she drank a mixture of water and rye though she refused food.

Such a strange thing, this giving birth. Sometimes it all went well, as in the case of his brother's wife. But you never could tell. There was that woman his mother had told him about, a relative who died in childbirth. She was young and healthy, too. . . .

There is no telling where the boy's thoughts would have carried him had not Gerasim just then thrown a log on the fire and startled him out of his slumber. Yawning and stretching, he rose to his feet.

'Wake me if you need me,' he said apologetically. 'Will you? I'll go and lie down a while.'

Gerasim reached out a hand to stroke his son's thick hair. 'Don't worry,' he replied. 'If anything happens I'll wake you without fail.'

Alone, Gerasim lit his pipe and settled more comfortably. His mind raced back and forth, seeking an explanation for the good and evil that were his lot. For it is common sense that everything has a cause. Take his life. There was nothing for him to complain about. He had an nice family. The two eldest sons were married, a third was in the Imperial Guards, in Petersburg, and Denis did well in school. His circumstances in other respects also were enviable. His granaries were full, and his pantries well-provisioned. In the stables were twenty fine horses and thirty cows, while two hundred sheep ranged his land. Yes, there was plenty of everything. Moreover, Gerasim was greatly respected in the village, indeed in the entire district. It was no chance that twice he had been elected elder. Now, however, though still in robust health, he was less active in village affairs and devoted himself chiefly to his farm, to hunting, and fishing. His taxes were paid promptly, and he had an excellent record with the authorities. Nor had he forgotten God, though he seldom went to church; on occasion he showed his devotion by lighting candles before the images of the holy saints.

There, sitting by the fire with his pipe, trying to drive off sleep, he thought of these things and many more and arrived finally at an acceptable conclusion:

'Of course there is sin. Who is without it? Often you sin unknowingly. Only a fool would sin consciously. Our kind, peasants, sin only when under the influence of drink. But how can a drunkard be held accountable? Yes, everything will be well if only Dowager will not disappoint us.'

While every evil must have a cause, he reasoned, if the evil that had befallen Dowager could be traced to no sin of his, then surely the outcome was not to be dreaded. His thoughts began and ended here.

At dawn the following morning, February 27, 1911, the hoped-for miracle took place, and Gerasim duly entered it in a small notebook in which he recorded important household events. It required no notebook to impress it upon the boy's memory.

He had been sleeping, when someone touched him roughly.

'Wake up.'

To his startled eyes the house appeared unusually bright. Everyone was up, although it was still dark, and there was a joyous murmuring all around. The family was crowded into the corner beside the great stove. Denis ran there, and squeezing himself between the crouched bodies, was just in time to see his father wipe a wet, black colt which was lying shivering on some fresh straw. Gerasim was saying in a happy, excited voice:

'God was good and Dowager did not disappoint us. Look what

a splendid young one she gave us. I almost missed it by oversleeping, old scamp that I am. The colt would have frozen to death.'

When he saw Denis standing there, his eyes fairly popping from his head, Gerasim shouted:

'He's yours, my boy. Come, take care of him.'

The words were like sweet music to Denis. Dropping down beside the colt, he reached out with his small hand and stroked the soft, silky head.

'Look, look,' he cried, 'what beautiful, fine eyes he has! See how he is watching us!'

Nothing at that moment existed for the boy but the dark-eyed colt. On an impulse he gathered the wobbly head into his arms, and the sudden rush of emotion he felt towards the helpless being was not unlike a mother's feeling for her child. Then he turned to his father.

'Father, how will you christen him? What are we going to name him?'

Gerasim stroked his beard and mused.

'You are right. We must give him a name. We ought to call him after his father, but his was such a long and fancy name that I can't remember it. What we can do to honour his father is to call him Jumper. He has his mother's colouring, but his legs are slender and strong, just like his father's. Yes, we'll call him Jumper. How do you like that?'

'Fine, Father. That's it—Jumper.'

While this conversation was going on the colt had gradually ceased to shiver. Lying there calmly on the soft straw, he turned his head first to one side, then to the other, and it seemed that nothing escaped his great wondering eyes. Yet certainly he had no realization of the joy he brought to these people who looked at him so intently.

Chapter 2

Jumper was born just before dawn.

The colt's first sensation, after coming into the world from his mother's warm and quiet womb, was that of knifelike pain cutting his body. Miserable but uncomprehending, he lay on the soft straw and shivered while something big and dark hovered over him, giving forth anxious sounds. He wanted to rise and press close to this creature in response, but he had not the strength. As the minutes passed and the blood congealed on his body the convulsive shuddering increased. He heard a distant noise of wolves howling, but was neither disturbed nor interested. He was conscious only of a need to still—to escape from—this dreadful shaking misery. Seeking protection, he lifted his head towards the creature above him, opened his mouth and whimpered. Then his head fell limply on the straw and he knew no more.

Some time later an abrupt noise wakened him. Indifferent, incapable of response, he gave no sign until he felt a pleasant sensation of something soft stroking his body. Strong arms lifted and carried him, and a delightful warmth enveloped him. He opened his eyes and was assailed by a bright light through which vague shadows moved. Some of the shadows approached and touched his head caressingly, making odd sounds the while. He was curious, but not frightened. The only important realities were the warmth, the sweet scent of straw, and a hazy awareness that he was the object of solicitude.

Now he no longer kept his head lowered, but sought to discover more about this new world into which he had been plunged. His mouth opened of its own accord, and it was not a whimper this time but an expression of confident satisfaction. In response the strange shadows crowded around, making loud noises that meant nothing whatever, patting his head, his back, his legs. Though he could not understand, he nevertheless knew that there was no cause for fear. The hands, the voices invited trust and he stretched his head this way and that, the better to acquaint himself with his surroundings. Had it not been for a vague irritation arising from a half-formed desire he would have been content. He wanted something. He did not know what. But swallowing the moisture that collected in his throat he experienced a delightful sensation that in part satisfied his need.

When a large and hairy object bent over him, wrapped him in something soft and warm, leaving only his head free, then lifted him and carried him outdoors, he accepted this new adventure as a part of the greater miracle. A blast of cold air striking his head caused his eyes to smart and momentarily he struggled, but strong arms held him close and a comforting voice spoke to him. He submitted and became calm. Instinctively he knew that the one who was carrying him could be trusted.

Suddenly he heard a loud and resonant neigh that seemed to confirm this knowledge: 'He-ee-ee-ee-aa! . . .' It was a joyous outcry which he instantly recognized as a greeting. With no less joy, though very gently, he answered: 'He-ee-ee-ee!'

As the colt's slight body came in contact with the great warm body of the mare, he turned his head and met her dark, liquid eyes. In the light of day they looked him over tenderly, anxiously. Then the friend who had brought him there stood him unsteadily upon his legs and, supporting him, pushed his muzzle against something soft and warm. Automatically he opened his mouth and grabbed, and a sweet liquid trickled down his throat, filling him with an incredible pleasure. This was the thing he had craved, this the fulfilment of his desire.

Gulping down the milk, lost in physical enjoyment, he twisted his little tail in delight and grabbed now one, now another magic dug. With the milk he absorbed something more and there was born in him an attachment for the mare. The caressing thrusts of her nose and her soft neighing indicated her delight at his touch, and how joyously she was feeding him. With his whole being he acknowledged her as part of himself—his mother.

When he had drunk his fill, strong arms lifted him again and bore him away. He heard the mare neigh—sharply, anxiously this time—and replied: 'He-ee-ee-ee.' The sound carried contentment and reassurance. He was not in the least afraid—neither of the daylight, nor of the white blanket of snow, nor of the varied noises and strange blurred objects in the yard across which they travelled. He gazed upon everything with uncomprehending but trusting eyes.

In a different but none the less positive sense the one who carried him, as much as his mother, belonged to him. In the man the colt sensed a friend, a protector, and he simply accepted it as a fact.

Back in the house, resting on a pallet of fragrant straw, he suddenly felt the overpowering weariness of utter contentment. Closing his eyes, and with his legs crooked under him, he dozed. Someone spoke unintelligible words above him but he even lacked the curiosity to open his eyes.

Soon he fell into the healthy sleep of a well-fed infant.

Chapter 3

The colt's education began on the very first day of his life when he learned the difference between cold and warmth, hunger and physical well-being. Cold was the great terror, and he was powerless to control his quivering body whenever the old man picked him up and carried him out of the house to be fed. After the brief discomfort of crossing the farm yard the sound and feel of his mother would restore his calm; the warm sweet milk would fortify his body. But though he felt at one with her, and knew dimly that it was she he cried out for when his stomach demanded appeasement, nevertheless with his hunger satisfied he was quite content to be returned to the comfortable room and his bed of fragrant straw.

These were the two poles of his existence in those early days: his mother, who gave him milk and expressed pleasing concern in a dozen little ways; and the bed where he felt secure against his single enemy, the cold.

Warmth and nourishment gave him strength. Confidence in his mother and the friend whose arms served him unfailingly made him brave. Within a few days he was able to stand independently on his long, thin legs and his firm hoofs.

With his growing strength was born curiosity about the things and people around him. At first he knew only that these other creatures made noises unlike his mother's familiar whinny and touched him in a different way. He regarded them with wonder for a long time but did not venture from the corner that was home. Then one day, when all was quiet, he rose cautiously to his feet and took a few steps forward, only to retreat hurriedly as a small, excited creature leaped at him out of the darkness with a tremendous whooshing sound.

'Cackle-ackle-ackle-ackle-ackle!' it shieked.

Jumper took time to recover from his alarm, before he again ventured from his corner. Avoiding his first adversary, he approached a soft-looking bundle of grey fur and touched it trustingly with his nose. To his intense amazement this friendly gesture met with a prompt repulse. The bundle sprang up with a furious 'S-ssssss!' and struck him painfully across the lip. Again he tossed his head, and took refuge in his corner.

This time he stayed there.

This incident taught him fear of the winged creature and the small grey animal. And fear in turn bred caution. He learned to distinguish among the unfamiliar beings around him, and came to know which of them he dared trust. Certainly, he had complete confidence in the old man who carried him regularly to his mother, and by meekly submitting to the caresses of the small person who so greatly resembled the large one Jumper soon became attached to him also. The boy's gentle stroking toch was pleasant, the mumbling sounds he made had some strange comforting power. Soon Jumper came to depend on his small attentions just as he did on the older man's care.

Usually the boy came to him alone, but once he was accompanied by a large, shaggy creature not unlike the deceptively gentle grey animal. Jumper cocked his ears in fright and made ready to run, but before he could translate his thought into action the dog gave him a damp caress with his tongue and waved his tail in a disarming manner. 'Vv-ow-ow-ow!' he said pleasantly, inviting the colt to play.

Jumper sensed that this also was a friend and not to be feared. Thereafter he came readily when he heard the welcoming 'Vv-ow-ow'. And although at first he merely suffered the dog's affectionate advances, in time they began to delight him. For they were a further pledge of security. They strengthened an awakening sense of his own power.

Once when he ventured from his corner, his hoofs clattering, the winged creature fled from him in fright. This emboldened him and he left the corner more frequently. Curiously he thrust his muzzle into everything, always taking care to avoid the little grey animal, and was pleased when someone reached out to stroke his neck.

Gradually his ears learned to distinguish the sounds he heard. One in particular, repeated often, seemed to bear a special relation to him. 'Jumper. . . . Jumper.' Whenever he heard it his head would come up, he would stretch his thin neck and cock his ears. He did not know that he was Jumper, but he recognized the word as somehow belonging to him, and he responded with his entire being.

These vague impressions clamouring for his consciousness and his growing attachment for the world filled every waking moment. It was a small world in which the man and the boy played leading parts. For their protective care, Jumper sensed, was not extended to him alone; it reached out to include his mother and the others—the large, shaggy, kindly animal, even the grey fury that had so painfully scratched his lip. It was, moreover, a peaceful, secure world.

The stronger he became, the more firmly he could stand on his thin legs, the bolder and more curious he grew. The close quarters in the house irked him and he widened his field of exploration. Now and then the results were disastrous, as once when he stuck his head into a white, sweetly scented mass, upsetting it all over himself. At first he could distinguish nothing through the cloud of white dust that filled his eyes and tickled his nostrils. He shook his head helplessly, snorted and beat the floor with his hoofs, until someone screamed, 'Jumper! Shoo!'—and with that he felt something come down smartly across his back.

Miserable, not understanding what it was that he had done, he experienced for the first time a sense of injury. His hurt was relieved only when he observed that his two friends—the man and the boy—were apparently not angry at all. They stood looking at him with merry expressions, making a noise that was like the voice of his mother. 'Ha-ha-ha-a-a . . .,' they chorused. And seeing that nothing threatened him any longer, he joyously added his voice to theirs with a resounding 'Hee-ee-a-a'.

That very day, upon his return from his mother, he suffered his first taste of discipline, without knowing that it bore any relation to the earlier incident. Every time he attempted to stray from his corner something stopped him by painfully tugging at his neck. He tried to break away but every effort to free himself only resulted in more pain. At last he gave up the exhausting struggle and returned to his corner, submissive but resentful of something he could not understand.

Now more impatiently than ever he awaited the coming of the big friend who would take him to his mother, and the visits of the small friend who gave him such warm pleasure when he rubbed his muzzle against the thin young shoulder. It was the boy, with his caresses and murmured conversation in which the word 'Jumper' frequently occurred, who finally taught the colt his name. Hearing it he would raise his little head proudly and with grave assurance. It was the first human word that had meaning for him.

Except for the limit placed on his freedom Jumper was content. The days were passing swiftly, it was getting warmer, and to his delight he was allowed to spend more time with his mother. This was a satisfaction because then he could drink his fill of the marvellous warm liquid, and return for more the instant his body cried out. While with her he was free to romp the length of the stable. He even surprised himself by rearing on his hind legs now and then or leaving the ground in a series of awkward jumps. For his mother permitted him these pranks with a dignified show of pride in his frisky ways. He disliked it when night came on, the stable grew dark, and the man arrived to take him back to the house. But though he resisted, the man was the stronger. And as soon as he had the colt fast in his arms his caressing, reassuring voice broke the resistance.

On the way to the house these spring nights Jumper's eyes searched the dusk inquisitively and discovered animals about the yard who resembled his mother; his straining ears caught the neighing of colts and other strange, exciting sounds that exerted an almost irresistible power over him. He longed to escape, to respond to these calls, but he could not. Back in his corner he lay on the soft straw, restless and vexed by the restrictions.

One morning early, when hunger told him that it was time to go to his mother, the man came as usual. But instead of lifting the colt in his arms, he pulled him with a rope towards the door. Jumper's first feeling was one of protest. This was unusual and therefore not to be accepted. He braced his legs firmly and shook his head in an effort to free it. Then suddenly he heard his mother neigh. 'Hee-ee-ee-aa.' It was a sound his ears easily distinguished from all others and it emboldened him at the same time that it diverted his attention from the matter at hand. With a bound he was through the door and trailing obediently after the man. As his hoofs struck sharply on the hard-frozen snow he experienced a joyous sense of freedom. Arriving at the stable door panting from the unaccustomed physical strain, he greeted his mother with a triumphant 'Hee-ee-aa-a'. It was as if he boasted that today he came to her of his own accord, on his own legs. Her responsive neigh assured him of her delight at his arrival.

That night the big friend did not come for Jumper and he was allowed to remain with his mother. Near her he had no fear of the approaching dark, and sleeping with his small head pressed tightly against her great body he did not feel the cold.

He never again went back to the house.

During the first hours of liberty he stayed close to his mother, satisfied to view the unfamiliar and somewhat terrifying world of the stable yard from that safe vantage point. But as the strangeness of his surroundings wore off the yard became a place of endless fascination. He thought he would never tire of it. When early each morning he and his mother were led from their stall, in sheer high spirits he would lift his curled tail to a jaunty angle, raised his head high on his long neck, prick his ears and romp madly—here, there, jumping, kicking his hind legs teasingly. He never tired of playing, and through all his antics was aware of a pleasing audience which included his mother, the shaggy dog who ran after him barking with furious gaiety, and very often his big and little friends—the man and the boy.

Everyone was kind, even the older horses regarded him with gentle forbearance, but though he feared none of them he never strayed far from his mother. Reaching the most distant corner of the yard in his joyous carousing, he would suddenly stop, turn his head towards her, and when he heard her warning neigh, run to her side with all the speed he could muster. Her concern when she sniffed at him gratified him. But though he understood vaguely that she would not have him over-exert himself or wander too far, he could stay quiet for only a short while. Then roused by something new and captivating, he would dart off once more, leaping and racing about the spacious yard.

This was his way of expressing the rapture of being alive. It was as if his small body with its grotesquely long legs were charged with inexhaustible energy. Beside him his mother seemed strangely—and to him, at times, irritatingly—lacking in spirit.

Only at night did he find rest, when after being locked in the stable with his mother he fed well and went soundly to sleep. Neither the dark nor the violent winds that blow from Lake Baikal in early spring had the power to disturb him. His body was satisfied. He felt secure in his world.

Chapter 4

The days were growing noticeably warmer now as winter retreated before the gentler spring. The air was so transparent that it was as if one were looking at the world through a magnifying glass. The sun's rays stroking the earth caused the snow on the roofs to melt, and cold, sparkling drops trickled down the walls of the huts and barns. With the advancing season Jumper and his mother were transferred each morning from the stable to a small open corral littered with fresh straw.

For the colt this was another step towards independence. The free open life of the coral intoxicated him and aroused in him frenzied outbursts of playfulness. It also gave rise to a certain dissatisfied yearning for a gayer world beyond. From his corral, which was on a small hill, he could look into other corrals of greater size in which horses and colts fraternized with unfamiliar animals with odd growths above their ears, whose 'Moo-oo-oo-oo' struck a depressing minor note in the assorted noises of the stable community.

To Jumper these meaningless noises were very disturbing. They invited him to become acquainted with the great living world, and his every nerve and instinct responded. Racing back and forth across the corral, he whinnied plaintively—partly from sheer nervous exuberance, partly because he was outraged that he and his mother were forced to live apart from all the excitement he could see and hear. When his whinnies were answered by the horses and colts in the distance his delight knew no bounds. The very air, charged with this joyous exchange of greetings in which he and Dowager took part, confirmed his vague consciousness of nature's awakening. Often in the midst of his play he would stop as if a hand had halted him, his neck would stretch to its fullest length, and breathing deeply through wide-distended nostrils he would gaze wildly into space.

Beyond the corrals lay fields, woods and hills still blanketed with snow. It was a world outside the colt's comprehension, but the vast space beckoned to him, promising something, he knew not what. As the days passed he grew increasingly restless, finding the corral as confining and as empty of diversion as the house once had been. The other colts in the great distant corral were a constant source of aggravation. If he could only join them, and show them his strength and agility!

His attention was drawn particularly by one colt—a small filly who never for an instant left her mother's side, and seemed always in a state of fear. Her unusual colouring—she was piebald like her mother—attracted him. But there was something else about her that pleased him and sent him cavorting arround his enclosure in an effort to attract her attention. He raced. He leaped in splendid plunges. He neighed at the top of his lungs. But in vain. The filly did not see him, or, if she did, she gave no sign. After one of these fruitless displays, he would resign himself sulkily to his solitude.

One day, when he had lost all hope, he happened upon the filly and her mother at the large watering-trough. There were many other horses there, but Jumper, having eyes for none but her, rushed impetuously in her direction with the thought of sniffing her all over and establishing friendly relations. The inquisitive, somewhat frightened glance she flashed him spurred him on in pleasurable anticipation. But suddenly, to his complete surprise, her mother stiffened her ears, bared her teeth and came at him in unmistakable anger.

Frightened and confused, Jumper flew to one side and sent a sharp 'Hee-ee-ee' to his mother for help. Instantly Dowager made ready to attack the piebald mare. She, too, stiffened her ears and bared her teeth in an evil leer.

The mare did not wait, and fled, to Jumper's grief taking the filly with her. He felt that his mother had failed him.

This awkward introduction at least made the filly notice Jumper, and from time to time they met at the trough. When he was in the stable yard he would push his head between the palings and watch her. His devotion was rewarded by her increasing attention, until at length she began to answer his neighs of greeting with timid whinnies.

Then a day came when, as he thrust his head between the palings, the filly approached him of her own accord. It was their first uninterrupted moment together and they sniffed each other with frank curiosity. The intimate exploration over, Jumper tore about the yard in wild joy, having an obscure wish to show what a glorious playmate he could be.

And now there was born in him a new desire—a desire to please. Behind his seemingly heedless antics there was a determination to impress, to win the admiration of the onlookers. Whoever saw him, he felt—the piebald filly, his mother, the other horses who watched him with indifferent eyes—must be made to marvel at his skilful cavorting. Now the caresses he formerly had tolerated became a necessity. When he saw the man or the boy in the stable or in the yard, even in the midst of play, he would rush to them, and wait impatiently to have his neck scratched. So greedy was he for attention that he trusted anyone who indulged him, and this strengthened the bond of dependence which linked him with man's world.

It can be said without exaggeration that Jumper was very pleased with himself and with everything around him. He was healthy, well fed, and had vitality to spare. Each day was an event to be greeted with new delight. Docile enough while in the stable, the instant he was let loose in the yard or corral, he seemed possessed by a demon, and he deliberately sought puddles, mud holes and other trifling obstacles over which he could leap easily to test his newly discovered strength. Dowager watched gravely as he worked off the energy acumulated overnight. Now and then an anxious whinny cautioned him against recklessness, but behind the maternal anxiety he sensed pride in his exploits. The presence of the man at these early-morning displays of strength was another incentive to show off, while the lame boy lent still further encouragement as he limped comically after him laughing and clapping his hands.

But Jumper was more than a playful young fool. He had understanding, and a talent for imitation. His mother was the one he looked to for guidance. She was as wholly admirable in his eyes as he was in hers, and he tried to copy her in every detail. This made them even closer than before. She not only fed and loved him, but through her wisdom and experience she added to his knowledge of the world.

He was right in holding Dowager in such high regard. She feared nothing, she never fretted, and she did not plunge and race like the other horses when they were being fed or led to the watering-trough. She was always sedate and grave. In the morning he looked on with her as the other horses were being harnessed to various contraptions and went dragging them down the road, guided by human beings whose nonsensical exclamations rose above the barnyard clatter. In the evening they returned, bringing fragant hay and heaped straw. Dowager's calm acceptance of all the seething activity that made up the life of the yard, taught Jumper something about the work of a horse. He came to recognize the leather trappings in which his elders looked so imposing as something familiar and to be expected.

One morning the colt was surprised to see the man harness Dowager and mount her. When they left the yard Jumper followed, running by his mother's side. On they travelled, passing strange buildings and strange fields. Horses he had never seen regarded them indifferently from behind fences. Fierce-looking dogs rushed at them barking. By closely hugging his mother's side Jumper avoided any mishaps, but he did not enjoy himself. Even when they had left the buildings and dogs behind and reached the open country his uneasiness persisted. There was space to romp, but he had no wish to do so. The vast snowy whiteness stretching out on all sides as far as he could see spelled an unknown danger. Urged to play, he only pressed against his mother and looked at the man with perplexed eyes. He was glad when at last they turned around and went home. The stable had never seemed so snug and inviting.

Yet that day Jumper had been made aware of something beyond his immediate experience. For a brief moment he had entered the adult world, and had progressed another step. Excited by the expedition and the vague sense of achievement, he attempted to munch some dry grass, and thrust his muzzle into a trough of crunchy seeds. The results were highly distasteful, and as he spat a mouthful of the seeds, he wondered at the pleasure his mother took in eating them. He still preferred her milk and the soft, deliciously fragrant pieces of bread that the lame boy brought him. And yet he wanted so to be like his mother!

Each day he waited for the boy, and when he came shamelessly pressed his muzzle against the boy's shoulder, and begged for the dainties. When, as occasionally happened, these treats were shared with his mother he was resentful and unhappy. For his ego was growing with his body, and jealously and self-assertion went hand in hand. He loved his mother, imitated her, depended on her, but he wanted to monopolize the attention of those whose authority he placed above hers. Already he knew that the big friend was master. His mother showed this in countless ways which he could not question.

Experience taught him that it was to his advantage to run promptly at the man's call, and to respond to his affectionate advances as well as to his commands. Playful and heedless though Jumper was, an instinctive wisdom told him that his life—as the life of all the animals in the yard—was wholly dependent on this human being, and that the requisite for their association was obedience. He could not help but feel the understanding that existed between the man and his mother. The man had only to speak and the mare responded. It might be only a twitch of the ear, but she never mistook the nature of the human words. Lacking a common language, she and the master still could impart their moods. The man carried on conversations with her as if she were another human:

'Eh, Dowager, that's a fine colt you have, and as frisky as they come. We did well to name him Jumper.'

The colt, hearing his name, would turn his head. Then, his vanity roused by the unmistakably flattering comment, he would take off with excessive zeal—racing, leaping, kicking, doing anything to gain the attention he felt he so richly deserved. His mother's voice pleading caution had no power to stay him. But as soon as the man led her to the stable, Jumper cut short his play, and went plunging after them with all the speed he could command. He was afraid to remain in the yard alone.

Chapter 5

A day came when Jumper's wish for a playmate of his own age was granted. That morning the master took him and his mother to the watering-trough as usual. But afterwards, instead of returning them to their separate enclosure, he permitted them to join the other animals in the large corral.

Jumper looked at the unusual and vastly interesting company, noting a few old mares, many young colts, an ancient sorrel gelding with wise eyes, and the shrinking piebald filly with her mother. At first he was quite overwhelmed to have his ambitions realized so suddenly, and surprise engendered in him an unnatural timidity. He clung to his mother, but his eyes were busy, and all his senses alert. Before long his shyness began to wear off. No one appeared to harbour any evil intentions towards him. Indeed, no one seemed aware of him. And when the filly ran to him trustingly his confidence was completely restored. He did, however, remember to throw a wary glance in the direction of her mother. It reassured him to see that she was grazing busily, and not showing any alarm on her daughter's account.

Leisurely, thoroughly, and with candid appreciation Jumper sniffed the filly from her head to the very tip of her small twisted tail. Then, on a sudden joyous impulse, he rose on his hind legs and spun round like a top. His flying hoofs scattering straw and dirt raised a dust storm of which he was the centre. The sorrel gelding cast a disapproving glance in his direction, but if Jumper noticed it he was too preoccupied making a favourable impression on the filly to let it bother him. That the filly was favourably impressed could not be doubted. Her dark eyes were filled with delighted admiration which spurred Jumper like an intoxicating draught. He forgot his critical elders. He forgot the manners expected of a newcomer in any gathering. He had only one idea —to excel in the eyes of this fascinating creature. He would surpass even himself, and perform feats of daring he had never attempted before. Determined, he rose once more on his hind legs and like an arrow shot from a bow made across the open space, punctuating his flight from time to time with a frenzied exhibition of kicking and bucking.

Arriving at the far end of the corral in a state of mixed intoxication and exhaustion, he stopped and looked around in triumph to convince himself that his performance had not gone unnoticed.

He was not disappointed. He had indeed attracted attention. Many of the company had stopped grazing, and looked at him, as if to ask: 'Where did this scamp come from?'

The effect of this attention was not, however, reassuring. There was something of a menace in the air, especially when the strange horses started moving in a group in his direction. Only then did he realize that he was far from his mother, that these strangers were barring his way to her. He felt helpless. Panic took possession of him and he started to run with all his might, hugging the rail fence in the hope of evading his pursuers. He was intent only on reaching his mother's side. Who would dare threaten him in her presence? He ran, straining every muscle, all his desire to show off destroyed by fear. But out of the corner of his eye he could see his tormentors hot after him, raising a cloud of dust and straw, and filling the air with the clatter of their hoofs, and with their angry snorting.

When suddenly several of his enemies appeared in front of him, cutting off all possible escape, everything seemed lost. Trembling, he stopped short, and shrank against the fence. But the host came on, growing more terrifying by the second. The colt could not guess their intentions, nor the reason for their hostility, but clearly their approach boded no good. So pitifully frightened was he that he coudn't make a sound to call for help. With his ears pricked sharply, his toothless baby mouth twitching, he waited for the worst to happen.

They were almost upon him. An ugly-tempered chestnut colt, teeth bared, was on the point of biting him, when he heard a loud commanding voice.

'Stop! What's this?'

It was his master who had saved him. At the sound of the voice the entire insolent, boisterous band scattered in every direction.

Jumper stood transfixed. The effect of the man's voice on him was no more amazing than the effect on his enemies. With his friend's coming all his fears were dispelled.

'Well, Jumper, you gave yourself a scare, eh? A little too lively maybe.' The man stroked him and spoke kindly, teasingly, and his calmness made Jumper feel that the world was again as it should be. He had only to look about him to have the feeling become a certainty. There were the horses, who only a short while ago were so frightening in their determination to destroy him, calmly munching hay as if nothing whatever had happened. With his entire being the colt was drawn towards the man who had brought this to pass. His faith in human infallibility soared.

How good-natured and harmless his recent enemies appeared now! Only the chestnut colt seemed to harbour a grudge. 'Wait!' his dark looks promised. 'I'll have another chance and give you the licking of your life!' But Jumper was not to be intimidated by threats. He was done with fear for the time being.

Filled with contentment he stretched his neck, blinking at the over-bright sun, and let the man scratch the sensitive spot behind his ear. When the filly clamoured for his attention with her familiar summons, he neighed happily in reply. And first one, then another answered, the voices swelling in a mighty chorus.

Jumper was no longer an outsider. He was part of the great community. And he was happier than he had ever been before.

Chapter 6

Jumper found the first day spent in the large corral exciting and pleasurable beyond his fondest hopes. His body seemed propelled by a secret spring that would not let him rest for a second, and inspired him to perform a thousand antics. When night fell at last, and the master led him back to the stable, he went promptly to his mother and clung to her dugs as if he were famished. Then having satisfied himself, he lay on the soft straw and closed his eyes in deep contentment. He was too overwrought to be able to sleep. In a dreamy half-consciousness he relived the impressions of the day. From time to time he shuddered and a faint cry escaped him. But when he opened his eyes the proximity of his mother reassured him. And from fitful dozing he at last drifted into a sound sleep.

Nights and days passed swiftly. Every morning the crowing of the cocks roused him from his slumber. Instantly he was on his feet, and, thrusting his head under his mother's belly, he sucked hungrily. The preliminaries over, he waited for the master to come and let him out into the corral. There, in the friendly company of his kind, he felt perfectly at home. The gay world he had regarded so enviously at a distance did not suffer on close inspection. It was all he had hoped for, and the very presence of these neighing, champing animals filled him with wild exhilaration.

His friendship with the piebald filly developed apace. In any adventure he undertook she invariably waited for him to take the lead and then ran meekly after him. If he attempted anything too daring, she merely watched him with gratifying attention. Remembering his early encounter with her mother, for a time he was wary of the mare. Also the frightening experience of the first day made him circumspect in his pranks, and careful never to run too far away from Dowager. But gradually, as he discovered that he was of very little interest to the others, he became bolder. He made the acquaintance of two colts considerably older than himself, one a large white youngster whose affable manner did much to allay his fears. Of his own accord he came and thrust his nose at Jumper. Words could not have said more plainly, 'Brother, you are among your own, so don't be bashful.' After some hesitation Jumper allowed himself to be sniffed all over, and after an irresolute moment he returned the courtesy. Both were satisfied.

Yet Jumper was not misled by these comradely demonstrations. Certainly the chestnut colt remained hostile, and showed no inclination of yielding. In romping about Jumper took care to give him a wide berth. He was dangerous. On rare occasions when accident brought Jumper near him, he laid his ears back, bared his teeth and looked so fierce that the young colt hastily scampered to his mother. With her at his side he could go anywhere and dare anything.

That Dowager was held in respect by all horses, young and old, was apparent to the most casual observer. Not one of them had the temerity to approach a pile of hay she was munching. And if she moved to another pile that did not belong to her the horses usually made way for her without protest. If they did not, or even if they showed the slightest reluctance to leave, she instantly became angry and as terrifying as the chestnut colt. When this happened Jumper could not recognize his kind mother, who was so infinitely patient with him. But though her wrath made him want to hide, her strength and courage filled him with pride. Following her, he never hesitated to annoy his enemy, the chestnut colt, whenever he had the opportunity.

His mother's spirit of independence gave Jumper not only a feeling of complete security in her presence, but led him to believe that such all-powerful protection gave him immunity from punishment no matter what he did. Fortunately for the others he was good-natured, and prompted by nothing more than his high spirts.

His favourite prank was to rush madly at some strange colt, rear suddenly, look challengingly into the stranger's eyes, and then, snorting furiously, dash off as if he were chased by the devils. This antic never failed to provoke astonishment and consternation, which he found amazingly gratifying.

The piebald filly made an excellent audience, though there were times when he discerned indifference, not to say disapproval, in her attitude. Now and then she even indicated a preference for other colts, among whom was the hateful chestnut. It made

Jumper jealous to have her attention diverted from him, but that she should tolerate his avowed enemy he found unbearable. He thought the broad-rumped colt ugly, clumsy, not as fleet, and, in fact, his inferior in every respect. To win the filly back when her fancy wandered, he resorted to the most furious cavorting—whirling, prancing, and kicking with his hind legs in the direction of his rival, though always at a safe distance. The chestnut was older and stronger, and his evil little eyes spelled trouble. But this only added zest to the situation. Often the ruse succeeded, and the chestnut, tired of his antics, left the filly to look for other diversions. This was all Jumper wanted.

Gradually the colt enlarged the circle of his acquaintances, being careful always to maintain the right attitude towards strangers—friendly but not too trustful. His observant eyes had noticed how cruel the older horses could be to the very small colts. But he disliked no one, except the chestnut and the old sorrel gelding with crooked legs and peeling hide, whose appearance revolted him.

This gelding was an ugly creature. Thick, green saliva dripped from his flabby lower lip, and his dim eyes were watery and filled with pus. Even though the master from time to time washed out his eyes and smeared the bare spots with ointment, his looks were not improved. He never mingled with other horses, and spent the greater part of his time lying in a far corner of the yard, indifferent to everything that went on, rising only to hobble to the watering-trough, or to nibble at the fodder. Even this was an effort for him. When, as frequently happened, a younger horse came and snatched at his hay, he at once relinquished it. Wisdom coupled with meekness had doubtless taught him the futility of fighting. Instead, he pitifully went in search of more hay. When he found it his toothless gums clutched at it avidly, and he gulped it down without chewing, so great was his fear of being deprived of it again.

Jumper could not understand such behaviour. The sorrel gelding was his first encounter with old age, and he was at a loss how to cope with it. As a rule he avoided the gelding as something beyond the pale. But one day, when he had satisfied his curiosity about everything within reach, he conquered his doubts, approached, and sniffed.

The sorrel did not move. He acknowledged his presence only by a flicker of the eyelids.

Looking at the disreputable old creature, Jumper hated him. Certainly the sorrel had done nothing to the colt, but he was a stranger in an otherwise happy world. His very presence was a threat. Of what? Jumper did not know. But in some way he had to express his fear and repugnance. If only the old horse were to move, he would not be so terrifying. How could that be done? This was not another colt to be tricked into play.

Then, as fierce hatred took hold of him, a surprising thing happened to Jumper. His ears turned and flattened out, his lips pulled back baring his teeth, and he rushed at the old horse—for all the world like his mother in a moment of anger.

The sorrel regarded him almost with indifference. 'And what do you want of me, you scamp?' his eyes seemed to say.

Jumper was about to repeat his lunge with even greater determination, when his mother appeared and smartly nipped him on the neck. This was the first time she had hurt him, and in amazement he jumped away from her.

The next minute he saw her sniff amiably at the sorrel. Apparently they were old friends.

After that incident Dowager took the ancient sorrel under her protection, even to the extent of sharing her hay with him. And so Jumper was taught to respect him, as well as to tolerate the ugliness of old age. He never bothered the sorrel again.

Besides, there was too much else to engage his attention. The very fact of being alive was a matter for excited wonder. Why else, now and then, did he stop in his play, stretch his head high, and, ears alert, gaze with wide-opened eyes into space towards the white, tree-dotted mounains that limited his world?

But when the rainy season began, everything changed. Jumper and his mother spent endless days in the stable. Time dragged with maddening monotony as, to the accompaniment of heavy winds, water drummed on the roof, and ran down the walls. It was not cold but the uncreasing wind and rain made the colt nervous. He stamped his feet, begged his mother for attention, and grabbed rudely at her dugs until the mare, unable any longer to endure his roughness, nipped him lightly to teach him better manners. Then, for a while, Jumper would leave her alone. Going to the stable door and thrusting his head between the stout bars, he stood disconsolately, facing in the direction of the large corral where, like shadows seen through a curtain of rain, some horses moved dispiritedly about.

Rain was not an enemy to be feared, as the winter frosts. But on his regular trips to the watering-trough Jumper hated the sensation of water pouring on him from the sky. It made him nervous and angry. Back in the stable, after stamping around and shaking himself like his mother, he enjoyed the luxury of straw heaped as protection against the damp cold. This was a pleasure unknown to his comrades who were outdoors in all kinds of weather.

For diversion he looked across the yard, at the stable which housed the piebald filly and her mother. But merely to watch her and exchange doleful whinnies was a poor substitute for play, and only increased his discontent.

While Jumper fretted from boredom, his mother bore herself with calm patience. She even seemed pleased to spend all her time eating and drinking. Certainly she enjoyed her hay and oats, her coat was noticeably smoother and shinier, and she became stouter and somehow more handsome. Snuggling against her, the colt was comforted even though, tormented by varied desires, he was unable to understand her placid contentment. Her indifference to everything except food was like the tedious sameness of the weather. Nothing roused her except the arrival of the master or of the lame boy. Then she whinnied cheerfully in anticipation of more food.

For Jumper their visit was the major event of the day. As he watched them busily spread fresh straw where wet, dirty straw had been, fill the manger with fragrant hay and the trough with oats, and clean and curry his mother, he forgot for a time his grievance against the world. If he came within reach they lightly and playfully ran the currycomb over him. The tickling sensation pleased him greatly, and, moving his lips, he stood quietly under their hands. Without glancing back he could distinguish between them—the firm touch of the master, and the lighter touch of the boy. The presence of those two, whom he had endowed with divine powers, and whose tenderness was as constant as his mother's, made him feel at ease and at peace with the world.

So the days dragged on in a monotony relieved only by the visits of the man and the boy, and by the regular trips to the watering-trough. In common with all the other inhabitants of the stables Jumper was waiting and yearning for something. He did not know what it was, but his mother knew, and her knowledge made her patient. For it was the same every year.

Chapter 7

What Jumper unconsciously longed for was the sun, which comes like a miracle heralding summer to Siberia. But first there has to be a depressing period of rain, to wash away the last traces of winter's snow and to ready the earth for a new and fruitful season. This was the knowledge Dowager had, and Jumper still had to acquire. No one could teach it to him, not even his mother or the master.

That year the rains persisted longer than usual. There came a day when the colt's discontent reaches a state of frenzy. In a wild outburst he dragged the hay from the mangers, stamped on it and sent it scattering to the four corners of the stable. When this failed to satisfy him, he stood on his hind legs and whirled like a top around his mother, until her outthrust muzzle brushed him aside as if he were a bothersome fly. He went to the bars on the door and neighed forlornly. Coming from the watering-trough he capered about in the mud and provoked his shaggy friend, the dog, to bark at him in disapproval. Finally at the end of the day, when dark obscured the familiar objects in the barnyard, and he was quite worn out by his efforts at diversion, he gave up, passively drank his fill of milk and lay down near the stable door, his legs tucked under him. His big eyes peered into the night, and his ears were ready to catch the least sound. Before long he slept, soundly, sweetly, and in his sleep he shifted his body to his favourite position, his legs and head stretched out to their full length.

'Coo-coo-re-coo. . . .' The doves were in full chorus at daybreak next morning when something softly touched the tip of Jumper's nose, and woke him. With a start he opened his eyes and turned his head, seeking the intruder, but there was no one in sight except his mother, calmly munching her hay. He searched again. Something unbelievably bright was penetrating the stable through the chinks in the door, and playing fitfully on the floor and walls. He watched charmed, and fearful that it would vanish if he were to move, and feeling instinctively that it presaged a transformation of magnificent importance in the world outside. A glance at his mother confirmed this, for now she had stopped munching and, ears cocked, was listening intently. Yes, there could be no mistake. Something unexpected and delightful had entered their lives.

Jumper sprang to his feet, and, imitating his mother, stretched his neck and with taut ears stood inhaling the warm, moist air. For some time neither one moved.

From outside came a swelling chorus: 'Peep-peep-peep . . . Chi-chi-chi.' It was a note of irrepressibly high spirits that had not been heard for many days, and Jumper quivered in response. Raising his head, he neighed loudly and long: 'Hee-ee-ee-aa-a!' His mother answered with a joyous call, and then from all over the yard other horses joined in.

Jumper began to turn and stamp, demanding to be released. Yet when the master came at last and opened the stable door he stood as if paralysed, blinded by the sun shining full in his eyes. In a moment, however, his vision adjusted itself, and seeing beyond the master the way open into the yard he realized that he was free again. The realization intoxicated him. With one leap he was out of the stable and careering across the yard, his head and tail held high. His mother neighed, and the master called, but he paid no attention. After weeks of imprisonment he experienced the supreme delight of giving his muscles play, and he was lost to everything else. Chickens, ducks and geese, adding to his excitement, scattered from under his flying hoofs, and mud splashed in every direction.

A call from his mother told him that she was going to the large corral, that he had better come along. The promise of seeing his old friends was even more attractive than freedom, and he bounded after her. The sniffs and snorts assured him that his neighbours were as pleased with the reunion as he was, that is all except the chestnut, who made it clear that he had no thought of letting bygones be bygones. Jumper had almost forgotten his old enemy, but reminded by the chestnut's angry lunge in his direction he retreated to a safe distance, and gave all his attention to the kindly white colt and the piebald filly. Especially the filly, whom he approached often, circling around her and performing all his tricks in his most winsome manner. He was happy to see that she was as friendly as ever.

The old sorrel was back in his corner, if possible looking even more repellent. Jumper went and stood over him, noting his peeling head, his dull eyes, and the spare sides with protruding ribs. Then he turned and ran off without so much as sniffing him once. The sight of the old horse was not in keeping with his buoyant, exalted mood.

With the beginning of Jumper's second season in the corral happiness seemed complete, and the future lay ahead devoid of all unpleasantness. Resting between play to peer between the palings at the blue-green haze beyond, he was faintly stirred by something calling to him. But the emotion was so vague that it did not affect his faith in the perfection of the world, or his role in it.

Jumper was too pleased with everything.

Chapter 8

Dusk was enveloping the land. The sun, a fiery ball, was disappearing beyond the hills, spreading as it went a wealth of colour that fell in sparkling drops on the uneasy surface of Lake Baikal. In the clear water of the lake were reflected the forbidding crags which crowded the shore and the distant hills covered with trees. The stillness that comes before nightfall had hushed everything, and the natural sounds seemed temporarily suspended; the call of birds and forest animals, the intruding voices of people, even the swish of leaves disturbed by the wind. The only noise was the gentle plop-plop of waves which lapped the shore and then receded, to return again and again.

On a sandy shoal fishermen, occasionally exchanging a few words, were completing their labours and spreading their nets to dry. One cart after another went creaking through the sand, carrying the day's catch to the village of Kabansk, until the place which only recently had resounded with stout voices and laughter of the peasants seemed deserted.

At the farthermost end of the shoal, near the water, stood the cart of Gerasim Ozerov drawn by Dowager. Strangely passive, Jumper clung close to her side, worn out by the excitement of the day. Except for Gerasim and young Denis all the family had returned home, but these two were reluctant to leave the beauty and quiet that spread before them.

The quiet of the evening had a disturbing effect on Jumper. For hours he had been keyed to a playful, holiday mood. But now he felt that the end had come. Didn't the setting sun put an end to every day's activity? He was ready for his rest, and it perplexed him that the others lingered. Impatiently he turned to look at his mother, then at the master, then in the direction of the village. His great dark eyes asked: 'Why are we standing here? Everyone else has gone. A picnic on the lake is fine, but home is the place to be at night. Aren't you coming?'

Switching her tail lazily, Dowager tried to make him understand that there was no need to hurry, that it was necessary to wait for the master's orders.

Added to the colt's boredom with this tiresome delay was his disappointment that the man and the boy paid no attention to him, although he was right there. In search for companionship he thrust his head under the cart, where the dog, on whose friendship he could depend, lay curled and asleep. But for once his friend failed him. The dog's growl indicated that he wanted to be left alone.

Disconsolate, Jumper went to the edge of the water and half-heartedly tried to renew a game that had amused him the greater part of the day. As a wave came in and, spraying him lightly, broke on the shore, he turned, and with enormous leaps raced to his mother, and then went back to the water's edge to wait for the next wave. But after one or two half-hearted tries he gave up. There was no more excitement to be had from this game—the fun was over. He returned to his mother and tucked his head under the curve of her neck.

For a time he was quiet. Then, as though he had reached a weighty decision, he gave a loud neigh. This had the desired effect. Both master and boy turned to him, called him, and, when he approached, put out their hands to stroke him.

Now that he was once more the centre of attraction he was satisfied.

'Eh,' the old man said, running his hand affectionately down the colt's glossy neck. 'He's going to be a fine horse, Denis.'

'That he will be,' the boy agreed with enthusiasm. Nothing pleased him more than to talk about his pet. He still marvelled and was proud that the colt belonged to him. With ill-disguised jealousy he added: 'He's much nicer than the other colts, don't you think? Kinder and not as wild.'

'Hee-ee-aa-a,' Jumper interrupted softly, and was not in the least offended when his friends laughed.

'You rascal,' Gerasim said, giving him a little push towards his mother. 'I do believe you understand what we're saying. Now get along. Such a smart colt might learn to talk, and then what kind of a horse would you grow up to be?'

Obediently Jumper went over to Dowager.

'You see,' the boy persisted. 'He is different. Why is that? Is it because of his father, who was also different?'

Gerasim was silent for a minute. Then he said in his grave,

ponderous peasant fashion:

'My boy, I don't know why Jumper is unlike the other colts. Maybe because of his father. But there—our own Dowager is good-tempered and as intelligent as you could hope for. She understands everything. And who gave her understanding? God and nature. So that isn't the reason. No, horses differ just like human beings and there's no explaining why. Some are clever, others stupid. Some are strong, others weak. So it goes. But one thing they have in common. That is a need for kindness. In that, too, they are like us. Take good care of a horse, feed and water it, and it will serve you faithfully. Never hurt it and it will trust you. Remember this. A horse is an animal that will not tolerate harshness.' He hesitated, then added: 'Treat Jumper with kindness. That is the way, and the only way, he will learn.'

There was perplexity in the boy's eyes.

'I don't understand, Father. You have to hurt a horse to train it. All the peasants say so. They say it is impossible to raise a good horse without a whip. They say an animal must fear its master or it won't obey, and that there's nothing that can be done about it.'

Gerasim answered him calmly:

'Much that the peasants say is true. You can win obedience through fear. But what kind of obedience? Look at them—they themselves tremble like leaves in the presence of officials. Is that right? I am an ignorant man but I have given thought to these things. I have lived according to the old ways. My superiors have punished me, and I in turn have punished others. Such was the custom. But in my heart I never approved of it. Eh!' he broke off. 'It's time to be moving. Come.'

He stretched himself, and said: 'Giddap!' The mare turned towards the village and set off at a slow, even pace. The man and the boy walked behind the cart.

'Yes, I am guilty,' Gerasim again picked up the thread of his thought. 'I have punished my children—all but you. You I have never touched. And what happened? You turned out to be the finest of the lot. There are horses, too, which thrive on gentle handling, especially horses like ours which are not wild. Take that old sorrel. He is more than thirty-one years old, and never once has it been necessary to use a whip on him.'

Gerasim paused and tugged at his beard, his forehead wrinkled from the effort to make clear to the boy something he felt deeply, even though it was only vaguely formulated in his mind.

'Aye,' he continued, nodding to make his point. 'A miracle of a horse he was. You could trust him with a child. He was a favourite with the whole family. Your grandfather told me before he died: "Gerasim, take good care of the sorrel, and under no circumstances sell him. He's a fine animal and does his work well. He deserves to die at home." And your grandfather was right. A kinder, cleverer horse never was born. As for Dowager . . . well, you have seen yourself how she stands unhitched, and won't budge until I give the word. A wise mare. For hunting there is none better in the entire village. She steps softly in the woods, and she is afraid of nothing. Fire a gun over her ear, and she won't stir. Nor will you ever get lost with her in the taiga—she will bring you out every time. In a snowstorm throw down the reins and trust God and her—she will never lose her way. Could you have taught her this with a whip? Never.'

Denis listened, his eyes open wide. Talk like this was close to his heart, as it is to the heart of every peasant boy. The human world he knew was intimately associated with the animals, but with the natural scepticism of a child whose daily life had shown him that the whip was far more potent than words, he doubted.

'Then how did you train Dowager, Father?' he asked.

Gerasim pondered, trying to pull from his mind something out of the half-forgotten past. Then he said:

'You can take my word for it, I used the whip freely on other horses, but never on Dowager. Why? Because I understood her nature. From the time she was a colt she was tame, and followed me like a dog. I had sense to know that she was a treasure and not an ordinary horse. I loved her like a friend. First it was necessary to teach her to trust me. After that I had to train her to wear harness, and to take orders. This was not so easy. In truth, some animals never learn. But isn't that true of children? And a colt is like a child. With one a kind word will do the trick, while another —punish him or not, it will make no difference: he will persist in doing what he wants. As for Jumper, he won't give us much trouble. You'll see.'

Denis was about to argue, thought better of it, and said nothing. He remembered how at a word from his father Dowager had started off for home. Something he had seen with his eyes merited faith

Conscious of the boy's interest and enjoying vastly his role of instructor, as well as the soothing sing-song of his own voice, which rose and fell in time with the soft plopping of his feet in the dust, Gerasim continued:

'Yes, horses are like people. There are all kinds—good and bad. Take the chestnut colt. He'll never understand anything but a whip. That's his nature. He is suspicious, stupid, ill-tempered, and cowardly. We'll probably have to castrate him. He'll do well enough for hard work on the farm, but not for breeding. For that we'll use the white colt and Jumper. Both should produce fine offspring. We'll train them gradually. First get them used to the bridle, then to a halter. After that we'll harness them with an older horse. Before you know it they'll get the idea and take the saddle.'

Denis nodded with profound solemnity and looked at Jumper, picturing in his mind the proud moment when, after the training was over, he would sit astride the colt and prance gracefully to the admiring glances of his playmates.

Jumper, unconscious of what his friends were planning for him, was frolicking. He would run a dozen yards ahead of his mother, return to crawl under the shafts, and now and then stop in front of the mare's head, barring her way. But as they neared the yard and he sensed familiar surroundings, his pace quickened and he showed less inclination to play. A fresh breeze was blowing from the lake. Stars, like candles, flared one by one in the darkening sky as night, fragrant and still, settled over the earth. Dowager swung steadily along, tossing her head with satisfaction, and deaf to her son's entreaties to hurry.

When they arrived in the village, Jumper stopped to announce his presence with the loudest neigh he could muster. A score of voices answered him from neighbouring yards: 'Hee-aa-a! Hee-aa-a!' For a brief moment he stood straining his ears so he would not miss any of those delightful sounds. Then he bounded in the direction of his own yard, the gates of which stood open. He knew that this was home, where he belonged, and where everything belonged to him.

Chapter 9

The spring days succeeded one another in a pleasant procession. Jumper felt that the world was perfect and unchangeable. Each morning his eyes opened on the same objects, and on the same companions, and in his youthfulness he took it for granted that this was all of life and that it would never alter. Even the ancient sorrel, so weak now that he rose to his feet only with the greatest difficulty, was an integral part of the familiar pattern. He was as necessary to the whole, as permanent, as the handsome, dashing year-old black mare, who snorted contemptuously whenever Jumper came near her. The past? The future? The colt knew nothing of either. He believed and lived solely in the present.

Then something deeply shocking happened.

One morning at sunrise, while he still was sleeping sweetly, as if in a dream he heard the other horses. They were making a snorting sound, but it had in it a note of fear that he had never heard before. He shot to his feet and stood trembling, with his head held rigid and his eyes glued to a spot towards which every horse had turned. There on his straw lay the motionless sorrel, his teeth bared, and his eyes in a fixed stare and unnaturally bright. The still body and the frantic clamour on all sides instilled terror in the colt's heart, and he crowded close to his mother, trembling as if he were cold. Here was a new, unknown threat, more terrifying because it had no substance. One must be able to recognize the nature of the enemy to be able to fight him. But death had crept into the yard and struck so slyly that there was nothing for the living to do. All that remained were the loose lips, the frightening eyes, and the motionless body. In that moment of fear the old sorrel commanded more attention than he had for many years.

After a while, as if moved by one impulse, the horses quietened, stopped their bleating and stamping, and moved away to go about their usual affairs. Nor did they look again in the direction of the sorrel, though the air was charged with an unnatural tenseness. The panic momentarily returned later in the morning when the master arrived with several men and dragged away the sorrel's carcass. Then calm was restored, and the incident forgotten.

This was Jumper's first encounter with death, the first intimation he had that life was a constantly changing process. It is not in the nature of a horse to remember and brood over a natural disaster. Until a similar event arouses similar emotions, a horse lives without thought of the past. So it was with Jumper as life in the corral resumed its normal course. Yet the experience left a mark on him and shook his youthful complacency. And when the sorrel's poor hide appeared in the yard for drying—before being used for shoes for the lame boy and other household articles—he sniffed it reminiscently. For a moment past and present met and mingled in his mind. He was acquiring knowledge that gives wisdom.

As spring advanced and everything became green and lovely the corral was pervaded with a restlessness, communicated to the colts by their elders. They munched the old hay listlessly, and called to each other with dissatisfied voices. Their senses told them that in the fields beyond the corral tender young grass was shooting from the awakening earth.

Nor was Jumper indifferent. Imitating his mother, he raised his voice in unhappy neighs and gazed into the distance, as his blood moved more swiftly in time with the excitement in the air.

Their senses had not betrayed them.

Early one morning the master opened the gates of the corral. Singly, in pairs, in jostling, eager groups they poured through the yard where several work horses joined them. Then they continued down the road until another drove of horses met them ouside the village. On they went—the older ones purposefully, sedately, the younger ones scampering in delight with their unexpected freedom. Jumper found it exciting and confusing. His head was spinning from trying to absorb the new scenery, and the din of voices and beating hoofs about him. At first he ran timidly alongside his mother, not trusting himself or any of his neighbours. But before they had gone very far he caught the spirit of adventure. Fear left him, he snorted to show his pleasure, and his head turned curiously this way and that, as his long legs carried him ahead.

Near a small stream the horses came to a halt, and as if at a given signal began to eat grass. Jumper imitated every move of his elders, experiencing the satisfaction the young know of being indistinguishable from their kind. He did not venture far from his mother, but he continuously discovered fresh sounds, tastes and smells that delighted him.

All day Jumper lived in a happy dream, exploring, renewing old acquaintances, and making new ones. By mute consent the horses from the master's corral moved together as one family, and accepted Dowager as their leader. As night fell Jumper's spirits dropped. He was satisfied with the day's roaming and eager to go home. The other horses seemed to share his feeling. They gathered in small groups from which strangers were excluded, and as the darkness thickened they stopped grazing and drew close to the campfire where the men were sitting. There they stayed all night, as though the fire and human presence offered them security. But Jumper slept fitfully. He did not know what he feared, but the sense of the great expanse all around alarmed him. The slightest rustling sound brought him bounding to his feet, fully awake and listening intently. His calm returned only when through the dusk he caught a glimpse of the familiar shadow of his sleeping mother, and smelt the reassuring odour of her body.

The nights that followed were less frightening. He became accustomed to the vast, silent darkness and to the strange, rustling sounds. The field existence was not a substitute for home, but at least he became familiar with it. Most important of all, by sharpening his vision, his hearing, and his sense of smell, it taught the colt many things. The field animals—timid, harmless creatures for the most part—had their own peculiar scent, and he learned that the nose could be an active partner of the eyes and ears in detecting danger. He discovered also how darkness exaggerates the least noise and the smallest object, and how a simple thing by day—such as an ordinary bush or a tree—becomes a spectre of evil by night. From his mother Jumper learned how to walk so cautiously at night that hardly a twig underfoot or a branch overhead was disturbed. When he moved through the darkness he paused to listen, to look, and to widen his nostrils, which caught any slight scent that might betoken danger. And from all the horses he learned that there was safety in numbers.

With the coming of daylight his fears vanished. He became again a carefree youngster with no thought beyond the pleasure of seeing across the green fields and eating his fill of earth's abundant offering. But, though he accepted happily this new experience, he was more than ready to accompany the herd on its regular visits home. Sensing that they were travelling towards the familiar yard and corral, Jumper put forth every effort to keep ahead of the others, and his spirits rose instantly.

The colt found something deeply satisfying in feeling himself a part of the herd. Because of that he was very disappointed one morning when all the other horses were driven out to pasture, and only he and his mother were left. He went to the gate and neighed disconsolately, protesting against such discrimination. But no one heeded him until at long last the master appeared to pat him and to give him a peace-offering of bread.

'There, there, Jumper,' the man reproached him. 'Are you a cry-baby? Let them go. We have something more interesting to do. Come.'

The master fastened the clumsy seat on Dowager's back, mounted her and set off down the road with Jumper tearing helter-skelter after them. Surely, he thought, eventually they would catch up with the herd. But no. At a near crossing they left the highway and took a path leading to the hills. Not understanding any of this, Jumper docilely followed his mother. As they approach the hills the path narrowed. Enormous trees and rocks hemmed him in, large birds with frightening cries and a noisy fluttering of wings flew out of the bushes, and the path grew steeper. He felt that it was a tiresome journey, offering few compensating diversions. Several times he tried to run ahead of his mother, but to no avail. An overhanging branch or some other obstruction blocked his way. He welcomed every time the master called a halt and gave them a chance to catch their breath. Though Jumper looked about him with interest he saw nothing attractive in the wooded hills which closed in on him. He had known only flat country with its open spaces, and here he felt shut in, and restrained.

After climbing some more the master dismounted, and led the way up a still steeper path, encouraging the mare and the colt with gentle words as he walked. Jumper disliked the excursion more and more as his legs began to feel like willow twigs and perspiration made him uncomfortably damp.

When it seemed that the torture could not be borne another moment the path opened on to a small meadow crossed by a brook. The master called to them to stop. Then he relieved Dowager of her saddle, wiped her back, and gave her a playful, affectionate push. Jumper understood that the unpleasant journey was over.

After a rest Dowager's first move was to drink from the brook. Then she turned hungrily to nibble at the grass, which was lusher and greener than anything the colt had seen. He, too, stuck his muzzle into the water, and was amazed at its refreshing coolness. He stepped forward until he stood in the brook, enjoying the feel of it lapping at his legs. And now, gradually, his usual curiosity was revived. He looked this way and that, but could see nothing but hills and a dense forest. He looked up. Yes, there was the familiar sky—a measure of comfort. Then he looked down.

Why! What was this? A colt. Overjoyed at his discovery, Jumper lunged to meet the stranger, but instantly the stranger vanished. In amazement Jumper stood still, looking at the spot where the colt had been. And there, miraculously, it was again, but once again it disappeared when he tried to come near it.

Jumper would not give up so easily. He tried a third and a fourth time, anxious as ever to make the acquaintance of the newcomer. Then when he began to be irritated by this game and by the stranger's coyness, the master and Dowager appeared in the water beside the colt.

'Jumper . . . Jumper,' said the master, standing at his side, and pointed. With the other hand, he patted the colt's glossy flank.

It was the single word Jumper understood, but along with the gesture it somehow conveyed to him a startling piece of information. Through some incredible trick the figures in the water were not strangers but a reflection of themselves.

He barely had time to digest this thought and return to the bank when his attention was caught by an odd implement resembling a stick which the master held aloft. All was very still. Then suddenly the quiet was shattered in a terrifying fashion. Accompanied by fire and smoke, a great roar came from the stick, circled the hills, and returned.

Jumper gave a leap—there was no time to think—and the next instant he was clinging for dear life to his mother. But Dowager was not in the least disturbed, and placidly continued her grazing. Her only concern was a swarm of flies and mosquitoes which kept her tail in a continuous, switching motion.

As explosion followed explosion she raised her head for a second and set her ears in the direction of the sound. That was all. Her calm eyes chided him:

'How can you be so stupid? Don't you see that it is only our master who is making this noise?'

Inasmuch as Jumper had to be in every way like his mother, it was not long before he, too, took no further interest in the explosions, except to raise his head and cock his ears. He had his reward when after a particularly loud report close by, the master gave him a piece of bread and patted him approvingly.

'You'll do, Jumper,' he said with satisfaction. 'I thought so. You're not of a coward breed.'

But though on succeeding days Jumper returned to hunt in the hills with the master and Dowager, he still was too young to enjoy it. He preferred the flat meadows and the companionship of the herd. Even the unfriendly glances of the chestnut were preferable to loneliness. Like any child, he resented anything that interfered with his immediate pleasure. He had no conception of duty and responsibility.

Chapter 10

It was midsummer. The days were hot, but the cool nights released the sharp, spicy fragrance of growing things and of new-mown hay that lay thick in the meadows. Jumper, as carefree and as happy as a child, spent most of his time in the open with the herd.

From time to time the master separated him and his mother from the others for a trip into the mountains, but these hunting excursions became less and less frequent, and the colt almost forgot his early distaste for them. Like inclement weather, they were something to be endured, and there was nothing he could do about them. For some unaccountable reason Dowager and the master derived pleasure from them, and that was enough for him. The fact that day by day he was growing stronger and did not tire too easily contributed to his forbearance. So did the knowledge that on his return he would be rewarded generously with dainties.

Now and then, when the master astride Dowager set out for the hills, he experienced a fleeting temptation to run away because a day with the herd appealed to him more. But he dismissed the thought almost as quickly as it occurred to him, and after hesitating at the cross-road with a regretful glance in the direction of the pasture he would dash after his mother. He never once questioned that his place was and always would be at his mother's side. That was one reason why he could be so carefree, because light-heartedness is a luxury that can be enjoyed only by those who feel secure. And to Jumper security meant his mother's anxious eyes, her broad, sheltering quarters, and her heavy abundant dugs.

At the close of the hunting season a new experience was in store for Jumper. Occasionally the master took Dowager away from the herd, harnessed her to a cart, and drove to a field where the earth lay in black furrows as a result of the ceaseless activity of other horses and of a crew of shouting men with whips. All this meant nothing to Jumper, but he let no detail escape his bright eyes. He found the procedure incomprehensible but vastly entertaining. The fact that the other horses—his mother among them—were tired and sweating from exertion did not for a minute disrupt his pleasant mood.

In his contacts with other horses Jumper was acquiring independence and a growing confidence. He was learning how to get his way and yet avoid trouble, as when he dodged the chestnut by hiding in the thick of the herd. For the most part he was received kindly, but now and then some horse took exception to his youthful arrogance and gave him a sharp nip on a flank. Then he had to twist and turn his way to safety. If that failed, he had only to whinny and his mother came flying to his aid, as he knew she would, no matter whether he was to blame or not. Was he not her darling? His entire life was based on this assumption. His position in relation to his mother was as firmly fixed as the position of the sun and moon in the skies. This was his faith, and, like any faith, it was vulnerable.

One night he was awakened rudely by the snorting of a strange animal, and as he opened his eyes, he saw a large black colt by his mother's side. Leaping to his feet, he waited for her to drive away the intruder. But to his amazement she made no move to do so. On the contrary, she seemed pleased. Nor did she make any move to protect him when he started towards her and the black colt rushed to meet him with bared teeth and his eyes shining with anger. Until morning Jumper was forced by the stranger to keep his distance, and he spent the time torn with jealousy. He had no doubt that he had lost his mother forever, and he was bitterly unhappy.

In the morning men came and led the black colt away, and all went on as before. His mother was kind as usual. Yet his fear persisted, and it was some time before he could keep himself from trembling at every unusual noise, dreading that the intruder might return.

The hours spent at pasture grew shorter now, and all the horses spent more time in the home yard. There was another, seemingly minor, change in Jumper's routine. On their return from the pasture he and the piebald filly were urged to stop by the porch of the master's house and eat out of a bucket a palatable mixture that was like milk and the bread he so enjoyed, and yet was neither. At first he and the filly found it distasteful, and both withdrew their muzzles from the mess with snorts of displeasure.

But gradually they came to like it, and to look on it as a treat.

They had no idea of the sorrow it was to cause them.

The master came early one morning, and motioned for Jumper to approach him. When the colt obeyed, the master threw a halter over his neck, led him to the stable, and locked him in. At first Jumper was calm though puzzled, because he never before had been separated from his mother. But when the last bar had fallen into place, the master had gone, and he could see the other horses leaving the corral for the pasture, he grew restive, and then violently angry. Was this a mistake, or a deliberate affront? Racing back and forth in the narrow stall he complained in loud whinnies, and heard his mother's anxious replies. But she did not come to him. All day he paced the floor and waited. Towards evening the master and boy came with a pail of the liquid he liked, but he would have none of it, and looked at them with sad, accusing eyes. Nor would petting and kind words comfort him.

Later, when the horses returned from the pasture, he spun frantically in his stall, calling and listening for his mother's answer. But it did not come. He was quite worn out by now and hungry, so when the master returned with food he ate. After that he felt better, but that night he was restless in his sleep. More than once he was aroused from pleasant dreams in which he was with his mother, only to discover that she was not there.

He knew that something had taken place that affected him profoundly. He had always been afraid of being left alone. This was real. His mother was no longer at his side.

Chapter 11

At first Jumper's longing for his mother found expression in continuous and noisy protests. He tore about the stable, beat the floor with his hoofs, and made the air ring with his frantic calls. In the morning and at night, when the other horses left for pasture and returned, he grew especially excited. Then his uneasy eyes searched the herd for a glimpse of his mother. After a score of disappointments his outbreaks became less noisy, and as his spirits flagged, his body, too, became drained of its usual energy.

From time to time the master or the boy let him go free in the empty corral, but he took no pleasure in this. Instead of prancing as formerly from a sheer excess of high spirits, he now walked or trotted slowly with short, forlorn steps. He would stand still for a long time, looking towards the field where the herd was grazing. If, as occasionally happened, a horse in the distance reminded him of Dowager he instantly became alert and, dashing to the fence, sent a tremendous neigh into space. 'Hee-ee-aa-a!' Then, failing to receive the familiar reply, he returned with lowered head to his dejected pacing.

Even his appearance changed: his eyes lacked lustre, his body became thin, and his once silky coat rough and unkempt. He did not refuse to drink his morning and evening portion of milk mixed with flour and water, and he nibbled at the fresh grass brought to him, but it was more habit than desire.

For several days his indifference extended to the master and the boy. Before, he had leaped whenever they spoke his name, or gestured to him. Now he merely turned his head reluctantly in their direction. Yet they were the only friends on whom he could depend, and the solicitude he detected in their voices and their caresses was a measure of comfort. Resigned and indifferent, he followed meekly where they led him.

When one day the master took him to the corral and let him mingle with the other horses, he hoped wildly for a moment that now, at last, he would find his mother. As if suddenly electrified into life, he made a circuit of the corral, in eager curiosity sniffing this horse and that. He found the piebald filly and her mother, as well as the friendly white colt, but Dowager was not there. So he retreated to a corner and stood quietly, his head drooping. Nor was he cheered when the filly came and ran her fine white teeth through his mane, though this was a caress he particularly enjoyed. His dejection finally discouraged her, and she left him.

It was strange how his loss altered everything, robbing him of his simplest pleasures and even of the strength of which he formerly had been so proud. He seldom bothered to neigh as the horses left for pasture or returned. Even the gay and friendly dog failed to rouse him from his apathy. Yet something survived of his attachment for the world around him. An inner compulsion gradually drew him towards his two human friends. They could not take the place of Dowager, but they were a source of affection and concern, and in his loneliness he craved these as surely as he craved food and water.

Step by step, he was being drawn more closely into the world of human beings. When he was led from the stable he refused to go off by himself, and stayed near the man and boy as long as they remained in the yard. Even in the corral, with all the colts of his own age about him, he preferred to follow these two as they went about their round of duties.

There was danger in this association, as there is in any dependent relationship, but for the moment it served effectively to restore his interest in life. Before long there was an unmistakable improvement in him. He carried his head higher, and was more alert in answering when he heard his name. On every convenient pretext he approached the man and the boy seeking their attention.

He was a favourite, and he knew it very well. This satisfied him to such an extent that he could do without the companionship of other horses for long periods of time without becoming restless. He liked to visit other colts now and then, but they were not indispensable to him as were the man and the boy.

He was in real danger of becoming spoiled when an unexpected incident diverted his attention from himself. One morning, along with the other horses, he heard persistent and grief-stricken neighs for an adjoining stable. The voice was that of the piebald filly, and Jumper immediately recognized in her cries the anguish of despair he had experienced only recently. Promptly his own voice rose in sympathy, and went soaring across the yard to his friend in distress: 'Hee-ee-aa-a.' There was encouragement and understanding in it, and for the first time in days Jumper felt an upsurge of his old energy. He knew instinctively that the filly, too, had lost her mother, and this sorrow they had in common was driving them together again.

Plunging about the stable, hurling himself from corner to corner, raising his voice in piercing neighs, and beating a frantic tattoo with his hoofs, Jumper demanded to be set free so that he could go to the filly's aid. Before there had been no purpose in his anger, but now there was, and it made all the difference. He saw the master in the yard and clamoured for his attention, having no doubt that it was within his power to set everything right.

At long last the master heeded the summons and came over.

'Hey, what is all this fuss about?' he asked. 'You think the lady is in trouble, eh? You think you can comfort her, eh? Well, maybe you can. We'll see.'

By this time Jumper was quivering with impatience and exultant that he had won his point. He had discovered a way to exercise power through sound. More eagerly than ever before he accepted the halter, and followed the master into the yard. Then with a toss of his head he dashed across to greet the filly, whom the lame boy was leading from her stall. They greeted each other with sniffs and little whinnying sounds, which expressed their grief and their sympathy for each other.

When the master brought them their breakfast, Jumper set the example by being the first to drink. With his muzzle buried deep in the pail he cast slanting, inviting glances at the filly, and when she, too, dipped her head to drink he switched his tail approvingly. Afterwards, their stromachs comfortably full, they stood thrusting their wet muzzles at each other, and snorting to clear their nostrils of the sweet-smelling liquid.

So it was that Jumper appointed himself the filly's protector. The role gave him a new importance which he greatly enjoyed, and the sense of importance restored his healthy vigour. To divert and amuse his companion he pranced about the yard with a fine show of his old spirit. At other times he simply stayed near her. And if he strayed briefly too far to suit her, her plaintive whinny brought him tearing to her side.

'Afraid?' his manner seemed to say. 'Well, you needn't be, with me around. . . .'

There was no doubt that she understood, and had complete confidence in this lean, long-legged colt with the proud drawn-out head and wise eyes. She was always calm when he was near her, and she was willing to follow his lead.

A day came when the master attached ropes to their halters, and started with them through the gate. Jumper followed readily, but the filly resisted. She side-stepped and bucked, until the obedient calm of her companion convinced her that there was nothing to fear. They were taken to a large, fenced-in meadow thick with grass, and with a stream running across it. There, with reassuring pats, the master let them loose.

'Go along,' he urged them. 'Some new company will do you good and help you to forget your troubles.'

They looked around, self-consciously tossed their heads because of the detested halters, and raced to a far corner of the field where they saw some of their old companions. One was a handsome and coquettish year-and-a-half-old filly. Another was the amiable white colt. A third—the disagreeable chestnut. The presence of the chestnut marred an otherwise happy occasion. On catching sight of Jumper he immediately assumed a hostile attitude, but Jumper took no chances, and attached himself to the white colt. The chestnut kept his distance, contenting himself with an occasional angry glance.

This ill-feeling was beyond Jumper's understanding. Simple jealously over another's affections, Jumper knew. Fear of being deprived of food was also a familiar emotion. But between him and the chestnut there was no cause for jealousy, and the meadow provided abundant grass and space for all. The senseless display of an ugly temper made him nervous, and put him on his guard. But even so, he took pleasure in the outing, and in the company of the other colts.

Nibbling the grass, at first half-heartedly and then with zestful appetite, Jumper and the filly felt their spirits rise. The lovely day with its exciting fragrances stirred their blood. When they looked up, they saw other horses in other fields, and in the distance the shining surface of Lake Baikal, lying at the base of towering mountains, and they knew that they were a part of a glorious world.

After this they spent many happy days in the meadow, returning to the stable at night. Their friendship with the white colt grew. Jumper made several attempts to become friendly with the handsome black filly, but her indifference made him abandon his attentions. She considered him an upstart, and was far more interested in some colts nearer her own age, who called to her frequently from across a fence. Whenever she heard them, she would fling her fine head to one side and run in their direction, her nostrils dilated and quivering.

Jumper disliked such behaviour. Besides, he forgot all about the black beauty when he noticed that the piebald filly was receiving the marked attentions of the horrid chestnut. This was not at all to Jumper's liking, yet he had not the courage openly to challenge his enemy. He was in something of a quandary, until the white colt came to his assistance, and of his own accord drove the chestnut away.

Enjoying friendship and the pleasures Nature afforded, Jumper and the piebald filly gradually forgot to mourn their mothers. They lived each day without thought or care for the next. Like all young persons they spent their childhood lavishly, as if it were certain to last forever.

Chapter 12

It was very hot that August, and August, as always, was the quietest month in Kabansk, because it was harvest time. From early morning till dark the village was deserted. Except for the very old people and the very young children, all took part in gathering the season's crop of corn, rye, and oats. Even the most irresponsible boys and girls knew that there was not a day, not an hour to spare. The peasants governed their lives by an old saying: 'The month of August furnishes us food for the entire year.' It was a time of back-breaking labour. Men, women, and children worked until they were exhausted, never for an instant relaxing their efforts as long as the fine weather lasted.

Jumper knew nothing of all this. He spent his days in the carefree companionship of other colts. For him each day began and ended with a pail of his favourite mash. His body was filling out, his mind was storing new impressions. If the older horses were not in the stable yard during the day, he noted the fact without wonder. In the morning and again in the evening there was plenty of activity. Without envy Jumper regarded the perspiring work horses back from a day in the field, or eyed the noisy cattle and the foolish, bleating sheep. He had no wish to exchange places with them; he liked things as they were.

He was not pleased when one morning the lame boy came as usual, but instead of taking Jumper and the filly to the meadow, led them to where all the horses were gathered in a great herd. Men came, and soon the herd was being driven from the field along a dusty road.

The horses went obediently, but now and then some of the bolder ones strayed and lingered to snatch succulent mouthfuls of grain that stood in sheaves, dotting the fields like monstrous buttons. When this happened the men would reach out with snaky whips and cries of 'Pigs . . . Devils,' and drive the rebels back on the road. From time to time Jumper, too, contrived to snatch a mouthful, and was pleased both with his daring and the taste. His mother had enjoyed grain such as this, and now he understood why.

Sometimes the horses straying among the sheaves tumbled and scattered them. Then women and children in the fields joined in the shouting, and dogs came barking. It was exciting. It was also frightening.

Except for these diversions it was a tedious journey. Jumper ran along easily, without tiring, but the dust that was kicked up irritated his eyes and nostrils almost beyond endurance. He, the piebald filly, the white colt, and the chestnut were held close together by a sense of strangeness and fear of getting lost. By now the chestnut had learned the need to tolerate Jumper's presence. He seemed to realize that the important thing was for all to unite against unknown dangers.

The herd was large, and it grew as it travelled until it blanketed the road for a great distance—a seething, many-coloured mass. Finally, after what seemed to Jumper a very long time, they turned off the road into a wide valley, where there were few people and no tempting bundles of wheat.

At a stream the horses stopped to drink, then split into groups and started to eat grass.

No one shouted, and no one snapped whips at them. They were free to do as they chose, and they chose to eat. After clipping the grass in one spot they moved to another. They were quiet and orderly except when the sound of human voices nearby, or the barking of dogs, sent them into sudden headlong flight. As they ran, their hoofs raised clouds of dust, and made a loud thudding noise on the hard, dry ground. Caught by the contagion of panic, Jumper always joined the others in flight, but he never understood the cause of this sudden fear.

Days went by and no one came to take them home.

The nomadic life of the herd did not appeal to Jumper, but he would have suffered much more than this for the privilege of being with the other horses, many of whom were now his friends. At night especially he felt his dependence on the herd, and particularly on a strong, dun-coloured colt whose duty it was at the approach of dark to run around with lowered head until everyone stood in a close, tight circle. Then he kept guard over them until day broke.

In that herd Jumper met his mother again, but they met not as mother and son. She sniffed him but remained indifferent, and after a moment or two he was content to go off with his youthful friends. And still her strength and serenity continued to impress him, and he frequently sought her out as they were grazing or changing pastures. Her calm gave him confidence. She never gave way to panic. When some danger seemed to threaten, and the herd took off in flight, she did not run with the others, but looked around and appraised the situation. She had a quality of courage and leadership that Jumper and his friends readily recognized.

One trait that Jumper shared with his mother was a sense of community with human beings. When occasionally the master appeared in the field all the horses fled, but Dowager and Jumper ran eagerly towards him, and they rejoined the herd only because he insisted. In a small way his devotion to the master communicated itself to the filly and to the white colt. Although they never approached the master, they learned not to run from him, and would stand timidly at a distance waiting for him to come with caresses, kind words, and possibly an offering of savoury black bread.

Every time Jumper and Dowager saw the master they extended their heads, begging him to put on their halters and to take them home, but he refused. 'No,' he said. 'You're a couple of rascals. You think you can get around me, but you can't.'

While this wild, free life did not appeal to Jumper, it made him cognizant of dangers that were made real by the eerie call of wolves at night. It was as a protection against this particular danger that the dun-coloured colt gathered them into a close-packed circle, with the youngest colts in the centre, and then paced around them on the look-out for enemies. He was a terrifying figure as with lowered head and ears alert, he kept nightly guard. His furious snorting served both as a warning to marauders and as an assurance to those he was guarding. Sometimes Jumper could see the shadowy outlines in the distance, their eyes glowing like pins of fire. Then his whole body seemed to distend with fear, and his long, thin neck stretched to its full length as he stared in fascinated horror. But with the coming of daylight the ghostly shadows disappeared, and Jumper forgot the horrors of night as the herd scattered over the rich pasture lands.

There was one other danger Jumper learned about. The chestnut colt had taught him that all horses are not naturally trustful and peace-loving, but Jumper himself was so good-natured and accomplished at avoiding quarrels that he had never found occasion to test his courage. The incident that opened his eyes to the cruelty lurking within his own kind was a battle between the dun colt and a black colt, who was the leader of another herd. The two horses had brought their charges to the same stream to drink and graze. With a shock Jumper recognized the black colt as the one who long ago had spent the night with his mother, and some impulse he could not have explained sent him running towards him. But the dun colt interfered, and himself rushed at the newcomer with shrill, angry neighs. They met, reared upright, and exchanged terrific blows with their front feet.

Now the conflict became savage. With their manes and tails flying the two leaders came together locked in a furious embrace, and separated only to come together again and again. Rising high on their hind legs they flayed the air, pounded each other relentlessly, and used their teeth. Occasionally one forced the other to his knees. Their cries shattered the quiet of the countryside. Both contestants were covered with sweat, foam poured from their mouths, and blood dribbled down their shoulders.

Shaken with fright and fascinated, Jumper followed every movement with his eyes, but did not utter a cry or stir from his place in the circle. So did the other horses, as with their concentrated attention they tried to encourage their favourite.

At length men came on horseback, and by cracking whips and shouting, separated the fighters. Otherwise the battle would have ended in death. Forced to break off, the colts ran in opposite directions to join their companions, and the incident was closed. But the memory of it, and its unbridled fury, haunted Jumper, and made him more anxious than ever to avoid quarrels.

The nomadic life was exciting, stimulating, yet it did not satisfy Jumper. When one day he and the other colts were separated from the herd and driven home he went willingly, feeling no regret for what he was leaving. Like a traveller returned from a journey, he settled back contentedly into the routine he knew and approved. It spelled security.

His closest companions were still the piebald filly, the white colt and the chestnut. They were as different as night and day, but they had this in common: they were fated to associate with man. In what capacity? The future was mercifully hidden.

Chapter 13

Late summer and autumn, with the warm days and brisk, cool nights, sped by. Jumper had everything to make him happy. But inevitably there came a change. Rain spread a curtain over the earth, high winds tore the yellowed leaves from the trees and scattered them. Then came frosts, and snow in great soft flakes returned beauty to the barren land. The long Siberian winter was under way.

At first Jumper was disgruntled to have to spend days and nights in a large enclosed pen where daylight never penetrated, and where the presence of many animals was the only source of warmth. But after a few trips across the yard to the drinking-trough he returned gratefully to the warm stuffiness of the pen. He hated the cold and wind, and the yard under a blanket of snow had an unfamiliar look.

Gradually, along with the other colts, he became reconciled to the inconveniences of winter. In this confined life small incidents took on a new importance. Now and then on the way to the trough he managed to escape the others for a brief, exhilarating romp around the yard. To prance about, with his tail held high, his ears pointed sharply, and his dancing feet scattering snow, restored his confidence and sense of well-being. With little else to occupy him he took note of every noise, and was fascinated by the variety of sounds. The happy calls of horses nearby, blending with the calls of cattle and sheep across the yard, told him every morning and evening that all was well with his world. In answer his own voice soared in a joyous thanksgiving.

The lack of space imposed an intimacy on the animals which did not exist during the other seasons. To Jumper, who by nature looked upon every living being as a friend, this was no hardship. Dozens of other bodies crowded about him gave out warmth and cheer. He came to like the noise, and to feel calmer and more at ease as the inhabitants increased. One day a herd of calves was driven into the pen, another day some sheep joined them. The timid calves, with their big, soft eyes, were especially good fun to watch. Try to come near them and they bolted. An odd thing about them was their solemn and businesslike preoccupation with food: they always were chewing something.

Frisking about the yard gave him some exercise but not nearly enough, and this was reflected in his encounters with the chestnut whose disposition also was not improved by the confinement. Although Jumper tried to elude his enemy by clinging to the white colt and to the piebald filly, an occasional meeting was unavoidable. In the perpetual semi-darkness, the chestnut's display of viciousness was even more provoking than usual, and Jumper, as he retreated to a place of safety, felt hatred as well as fear rise inside him. These encounters became more frequent as time went on and the cold kept them prisoners. Once Jumper caught a hard blow from the chestnut's hoofs. Another time the chestnut bit him cruelly on the back and haunches. Jumper stood the indignities, not knowing how to retaliate, but he was discovering what it is to hate.

As the shortening days went by, and the bitter Siberian winter beat on the stable walls, sending spears of cold through every crack, the hardships of this indoor life made themselves felt more and more. An animal, like a human being, must have interests beyond eating and sleeping. A restlessness pervaded the stable. An unexpected move by any horse was likely to irritate the others, and to set the whole place in a turmoil. The piebald filly, usually so good-natured, decided that she disliked the calves and sheep, and every time they came near her she turned on them in a temper and sent them scurrying. Several times the amiable white colt, without any provocation, attacked the chestnut, and since the chestnut had little or no chance against this opponent he retreated, and took his anger out on Jumper.

A day came when Jumper could stand it no longer. They were just returning to the pen after their morning trip to the watering-trough when the chestnut made a sudden, savage, and unprovoked attack. Jumper was still exhilarated by the dash around the yard, and the taste of delicious black bread given him by the master was strong in his mouth. He was in a most contented mood, far from any thought of a quarrel. For that reason he resented the chestnut's intrusion more than usual. There was no time to think or to escape when he suddenly found himself in a corner with the enemy barring the way to safety. In that instant something tremendous happened. A ball of fire seemed to gather within him, speed along every nerve of his body, and burst somewhere in his head. Incensed, he turned and let fly with both hind legs. Then, before his tormentor had time to recover from pain and astonishment, he faced him, flattened back his ears, and lunged. By now, along with the fury, Jumper felt a satisfying sense of power, and he was determined to settle matters with the chestnut once and for all. But to his amazement, instead of advancing to meet him, the chestnut gave ground. The battle so unexpectedly begun was just as unexpectedly over.

After that Jumper had no reason to avoid the chestnut. He walked up to him whenever he felt so inclined, and looked at him boldly, enjoying the knowledge that it was the chestnut who now was uneasy. The victory so quickly won did not make him pugnacious because he was too friendly and trusting by nature, but by dispelling his fear it changed his status among his companions. He no longer was one of the hunted; instead he had qualified to assume the role of a protector. He was now a year old, and had a great deal of strength and independence.

Even before man was sure that the sun was stronger, and the days longer, Jumper and the other animals sensed it, and there was a different note in the calls they sent soaring above the barnyard. Each long-drawn neigh was a plea for release from the tedious cold and gloom of winter and from the crowded, evil-smelling stable.

A day came at last when the master led all the colts to an open corral and set them free. Jumper was beside himself with happiness, because this meant more than just an opportunity to play and stretch his muscles, so weary of inactivity. It meant that, despite the piles of snow that lay everywhere, spring was finally near. Raising his head high, and drinking the keen air through distended nostrils, he seemed to recall that other spring and summer with all the delights they had held.

How differently he had greeted his first spring—weak, timid, uncomprehending, clinging to his mother's side for protection against dangers he did not know. Now he was strong and fearless, and he looked to no one for protection. While his friendship with the piebald filly and the white colt gave him as much pleasure as ever, he was less dependent on them. He romped as he pleased, and ate from any pile of hay that took his fancy, knowing that he was capable of defending his rights without outside help.

A sensation he enjoyed was to stand with his legs spread wide, and his head resting on the top bar of the fence, and look across the fields. Only an adult horse could do this. Before he always had had to peer between the bars.

Actually he was not as big or as strong as the white colt with his broad quarters, or as the barrel-shaped chestnut, though he looked taller because of his long, lean build. And something about his confident manner, and his calm assumption that nothing he did could be wrong, gave him authority in the eyes of his companions. Even those who could win over him in a fight let him have his way. He was different—set apart by his appearance, his agile, playful ways, and his strange bond with the human beings.

The sense of power was a glorius discovery but it did not mean that he was independent. Jumper's need of human beings was a real as his need of the sun. Their care and affection had given him a happy childhood. He took it for granted that the days to come would be as carefree.

PART II

Chapter 14

Jumper greeted his second spring and summer with confidence and zest. Roaming the fields and forests under no compulsion except to satisfy his hunger, swimming with the herd in the rivers that crossed their path, he accepted each experience as something marvellously new. Within the herd he lived close to his tested friends, the piebald filly and the white colt, and there were hundreds of others whom he encountered briefly, enjoyed and then forgot. One day the master came leading his mother, Dowager, but neither was particularly interested. They sniffed each other in polite greeting and turned away. Jumper no longer had need for the mare, and she in turn seemed to agree that he was grown up and capable of arranging his own life.

For all its abundance, life with the herd had its share of unpleasant incidents. One day, as Jumper was walking through a thicket, a thorny branch caught him and gashed him in the flank and groin. The pain was not severe, but the wound was an invitation for flies, gnats, and every prowling insect to worry and torture him. He was miserable, and with each day his misery increased, until his very existence became intolerable.

As always, it was the master who came to his rescue, and set things to rights again.

'Tsk-tsk-tsk,' the master said when he came to look over the herd, and saw Jumper's wound. 'What is this? I think you'll have to come home with me, my fine fellow.'

So Jumper returned to the stable. There his wounds were washed and covered with an evil-smelling ointment, which kept the insects from bothering him. The master came daily to treat him. At first even the touch of water was painful, and he struggled to free himself of the man's gentle grasp. But finding that this was impossible, he submitted and gradually became calm. As the pain lessened, he came to understand dimly that the discomfort of the treatment was somehow associated with his well-being, and that the master was rendering him a service. After that he did not move while his wounds were being dressed. Only occasionally he turned his head to watch the master and the lame boy, and perhaps playfully to try to reach them with his lips.

When his wounds were healed Jumper's usual contented mood was restored in the familiar surroundings. True, he missed the companionship of other colts. When he saw a horse in the distance, he became excited and neighed loudly to attract attention, but his solitude did not last long. One evening the master arrived in the yard with the piebald filly, the white colt, and the chestnut, and then Jumper was completely happy. For long stretches of time he stood head to head with his friends—first with the filly, then with the white colt—as they tenderly rubbed each other's withers with their teeth. This was their favourite way of expressing friendship. The chestnut seldom was accepted on such an intimate footing, but he gave them no trouble, and was treated in return with distant politeness.

Jumper had nothing more to desire, and yet, as the summer advanced, a vague restlessness possessed him. His even temper became ruffled on the slightest provocation. The cause of this inward disturbance was the piebald filly. Jumper did not like to see her play with other colts, and when one came near her he became terribly upset. He was able to handle the chestnut with scant courtesy, but because of their old friendship the white colt required more subtle treatment. Whenever he and the filly came together, Jumper managed to squeeze between them, and to draw their attention to himself. He had no conception of jealousy, and he vaguely understood that he had no quarrel with the white colt, but still he insisted on monopolizing the filly.

A crisis in the relationship of the colts seemed imminent when something so dramatic occurred that it thrust everything else aside for the moment.

One day they were driven into a small corral where there was a log bonfire. Beside it stood the master holding an iron rod, the tip of which glowed red, and beyond him a number of older colts in an excited knot. The colts were terrified: they trembled, snorted, and rolled their eyes, and whenever one of the men came near them they bolted to a far corner of the enclosure. Despite the confusion they were caught one by one, tied, and left to watch the proceedings around the fire. They anticipated something unpleasant, but they could not guess what it was, and their lack of knowledge frightened them even more.

Inevitably the common fear communicated itself to Jumper. He looked at everything with startled eyes, and from time to time was seized by violent fits of trembling. The presence of the master gave him reason to believe that he had nothing serious to fear, and so he did not tug and toss like the other colts. That is, he did not until a man came and untied the chestnut, threw him on the ground, bound him, and the master pressed the evil glowing rod to his haunch. Then Jumper knew real panic. The horrid smell of burning hair and flesh assailed his nostrils, while a wildly plaintive neigh beat on his ears. He saw the chestnut heave to one side and strike out with his legs in an effort to get free, and he saw the terror in the eyes of the colt when the master with a knife in his hand approached him a second time, and deftly slit his ear.

After the chestnut colt was released, the white colt and the piebald filly were thrown to the ground. The men went through the same mysterious performance while distressed cries continued to rend the air. With foreboding Jumper saw that as his playmates were freed to join the other horses, their haunches quivered strangely, something red dripped from their ears, and they tossed their heads as if in pain.

Now it was his turn. The master untied and led him towards the fire. He spoke cheerfully, and his touch was caressing. 'Whoa, Jumper,' he said. 'Steady, boy.'

Jumper was frightened, but as long as the master was near he could not believe that any evil could befall him. He shivered as if he were chilled, but he offered no resistance—even when he was thrown and bound. Only when he felt a stinging pain in his ear and haunch did he cry out or attempt to struggle.

'Hee-ee-ee!' His voice was a shrill protest.

The pain in his haunch was particularly sharp, but even worse was the realization that the master whom he trusted had betrayed him.

Almost immediately he was untied, and stumbling to his feet, he plunged seeking protection into the very centre of the herd of colts. The pain was nearly gone, but the fear persisted—a fear of strange, unknown things to come. When the fire was put out, and the glowing iron removed, he felt slightly reassured.

The master and the lame boy approached, stroked him, and offered him pieces of the tasty bread he loved.

'Good boy, Jumper,' the man said. 'Come. Forgive us.'

Jumper understood that he was being praised, though he did not know why. He wanted the bread, but he was afraid.

'Ee-ee-ee,' he replied softly, reproachfully.

He could not forget the betrayal so readily. Yet the man's gestures were friendly, and Jumper wanted the bread very much.

Gradually his confidence in his friend returned. The memory of many kindnesses dispelled his doubts. Yes, for some unaccountable reason the master had hurt him, but with no intention of making him suffer. As the pain lessened, the incident became a shadowy memory. But his first experience with pain left one permanent scar—a circle on his right haunch and a pronged left ear—the two brands which for many years had served to identify the horses belonging to the Ozerov family.

Chapter 15

With the return of winter Jumper was again confined to the stable, and this time only with the white colt for company. This in itself was a bore, but the principal cause of his dissatisfaction was the separation from the piebald filly. The white colt also suffered for the same reason. If they had not been able to see the filly at all, they might have forgotten her, because their memories were short and they lived only in the present. But every day they saw her in the distance, though they were not permitted to approach her. This was intolerable, and they neighed, pawed the ground, twisted, turned, and plunged in protest, until one of the workmen, losing patience, would shout: 'Hey, you overfed devils, what's got into you? Stop that noise before I give you a taste of the whip. That'll teach you.' They didn't have to understand the words to recognize a threat, and for a while they would subside.

This winter was not like the preceding winter, spent in the overcrowded, semi-dark barn among the strangely assorted company of animals. Then they had had a minimum of care, but all the companionship their hearts could desire. Now they were pampered, and lived in lonesome luxury. There was plenty of air and light in the spacious quarters, fresh, fragrant straw rustled under their feet, the mangers always were filled to overflowing with hay, and every morning, after being watered, they were curried within an inch of their lives. This was their chief diversion, and, while they stood tethered to their posts, they watched enviously the activity in the yard.

Because of the care and the good food, Jumper's dark coat became smooth and glossy. Usually it was the master who worked on him, using the currycomb and brush in firm, even strokes and talking to him the while.

'You're a handsome lad, Jumper,' he teased. . . . 'Eh! So you know it'—he added as Jumper shifted his weight from one leg to another, stretching his long neck, whinnying, and obviously showing off for all the world to see.

Or:

'Tut-tut! Have you never heard that the vain are the first to fall? Now stop admiring yourself and let's get on with this business.'

The words had no meaning to Jumper, but the playful, caressing voice meant everything. This daily ceremony was something of a game, and whether the master or the horse enjoyed it most is difficult to say.

The white colt, on the contrary, found no pleasure in being curried. The labourers who looked after him were not too gentle, and before they had finished they were sure to be shouting and cursing. Like most good-natured people, the white colt was indolent and slovenly. He had a habit of lying down in filth which left unsightly traces, and his stout flanks invariably were stained with splotches of yellow difficult to remove.

On occasions, the master tied Jumper behind a sleigh or to the shaft of a sleigh drawn by a large, placid chestnut sorrel, and they would drive beyond the village into the open country. There the colt would be seized with a desire to be free, and to race through snow-covered space, but leather straps held him fast. So after tossing his head, and prancing irritably he was forced to adjust himself to the jog of his lazy middle-aged companion.

There was nothing to see on these trips but unbroken fields of snow, nothing to hear but the screech of the sleigh's runners on the frozen ground. Though the monotony of the slow pace set by the other horse wearied him, he returned home in bouncing spirits and with an appetite that threatened to impoverish the master.

At first Jumper merely reconciled himself to these jaunts, but in time he came to like them.

The master gave him a great deal of his time, and continued to make each day a little different from the one before. There was the day, for instance, when Jumper was surprised to discover in his mouth a cold piece of metal which cut his lips at the lightest pull of the reins, and which compelled him to turn this way or that at the master's will. He was made to circle round and round at the end of a long rope.

'Tchk, tchk,' the master gave him the signal. 'Giddap. . . . Faster! Faster! . . . Whoa!'

The lame boy watched, delighted, and clapped his mittened hands. 'That's it, Jumper, that's it. You are a beauty!'

Even the dog took a part in the proceedings by racing alongside and barking furious encouragement.

Jumper, who liked nothing better than to be the centre of admiring attention, found all this wonderfully exciting. To please his audience and to gratify himself he ran willingly, with haughty grace, just as long as it was demanded of him. Then, to the noisy acclaim of his friends, he received his reward—pieces of the soft and tasty bread he loved.

Like a schoolboy eager for more interesting lessons, Jumper hungered to learn more and more, and to display his new accomplishments.

One day the master led him and the white colt into the large corral, and, after tying them to a post, placed on their backs pads which fastened with straps under their bellies. At the first tug the white colt protested violently, whirling and rearing, and, when that failed to remove the obnoxious tightness, in fury he struck out with his hind legs. Jumper was puzzled, but not alarmed. The strap tickled, and he shuddered, but it was nervousness rather than fear.

After several days of this, when he was accustomed to the feel of the pad on his back, the master surprised him by tossing a heavy piece of leather on top of the pad. Quickly he tightened the strap, but not before Jumper had puffed his body into a hard knot. This was more than he had bargained for: an affront to his dignity, and an imposition which even his good nature could not endure. He was ready to plunge.

'Now, now,' he heard the master's soothing voice. 'There is nothing to be afraid of. What could hurt you? A saddle? Ho! What is a saddle to a fine, strong fellow like you?'

The words meant nothing, but the quiet tone in which they were spoken broke up Jumper's intention to rebel. He swelled himself a size larger and pranced a little to assert his independence. But the saddle remained on his back, and nothing unpleasant happened.

The next day he accepted the saddle more calmly, and after that it became a routine procedure.

One morning several days later the lame boy came to the stable. Willingly Jumper followed him to the large corral, thrust out his muzzle to receive the bridle, and allowed the saddle to be placed on his back. The boy had bread with him, which Jumper ate with relish, as he stood by a large stone.

Was the bread a payment for some service not yet rendered? Jumper never looked that far ahead. The bread was delicious, and simply indicated that he was in favour with his friends.

Then came a sudden shock as with one swift movement the boy landed squarely on his back, holding the reins in such a way that the bit cut painfully into his lips. Jumper was terrified beyond all reason, and did the first thing that his instinct prompted him to do. He rose on his hind legs and, turning sharply, bolted across the corral. Having reached the far side he found that the boy still was on his back. To rid himself of the burden he turned again, lowered his head, and kicked. Now there was no one on his back.

Having accomplished his purpose, he stood quietly and looked about him. Some distance away the boy sat on the ground, laughing, beckoning, and holding out some bread.

'Come on, Jumper, come and get it. How funny you look! I surprised you, didn't I? Well, you surprised me too.' This was the voice the boy always used when they were playing games. Apparently, carrying the boy on his back was just another game.

After only a slight hesitation Jumper went over to the boy, who was now on his feet, and accepted the bread.

The game was repeated every day, and Jumper protested less and less. When he obeyed the reins, as he learned to do, everything went well, and he suffered no discomfort. Moreover, he was showered with caresses and attention, which he enjoyed quite as much as the bread that accompanied them. But whenever he attempted to rebel everything went wrong. His mouth hurt, and the few caresses he received were given him grudgingly. Jumper was far too intelligent not to draw conclusions. Acting on his understanding, as time passed, he grew more and more tractable.

Besides becoming obedient, he also was learning that the queer sounds made by human beings had meaning. He had known his name for a long time. Now he recognized other words and occasional phrases. 'Giddap' and 'Whoa' were the most common. He knew when a tug at the reins meant a left or a right turn. Above all, he knew when he was being praised or scolded.

The tenderness that was shown him he repaid in kind. When he was loose in the yard he tagged after the master and the boy, and nuzzled them when they stood near, as if to say: 'I am yours and my life is yours. You can trust me. I will do anything you ask me.'

His faith in human beings was supreme, he had no fear of them, and he never questioned their wisdom.

Chapter 16

Jumper was fully aware that he was quite the best pupil among the colts of his age, and the knowledge made him proud. None of the others obeyed as willingly. Certainly not the chestnut, who kicked and whinnied angrily and offered every kind of resistance he could devise whenever the men tried to harness him. Even the white colt, who in most matters was good-natured and docile, showed stubborn resistance. For their pains these two were cursed and beaten—especially the chestnut, who obeyed nothing but force.

By the time Jumper was two years old he could carry a rider, or draw a light sleigh with only the guidance of reins. Also, he could be teamed safely with another horse. At times he was skittish and playful. When he was led from the stable he assumed that the day was planned for his special enjoyment, and he cut every imaginable caper. But this was only an exuberance of spirits. As soon as the harness was brought he submitted readily, and settled to the performance of his duties.

The master and boy took turns exercising him. Very often they harnessed him to the sleigh, and followed snow-covered roads to Lake Baikal, where he was free to run. This was exciting, because he could rush across the frozen, glossy surface, and stretch his legs to their fullest. Now and then he over-exerted himself and faltered in his pace. Then his driver would warn him by pulling on the reins.

Running always was an exhilarating pleasure, but he preferred above all else the races in which he and the boy competed against other colts and boys of their age. Saddles were never used. The boy rode bareback, and they headed out of the village for a level stretch of road where a merry, boisterous group waited, filling the air with boasts.

'You never did.'

'I did too.'

'Well, you can't do it again.'

'Who says I can't?'

'Oh, go on.'

And then the race—the thundering hoofbeats and the laboured breathing of the rival horses crowding beside him, and the shrill voices of the boys urging them on.

'Come on, Beauty.'

'Give it a little more, Blackie.'

'Show'em what you can do, Lucky.'

'Hi-yi! Eeeeee!'

Intoxicated by the noise and excitement, Jumper knew nothing but the urgency of out-distancing every horse on the field. And more and more often he came out the winner. There were other horses as swift or swifter at the start, but none could touch him in endurance. The longer the course, the greater were his chances of winning, because his sweeping leaps were never a drain on his strength. Once he had reached his maximum speed he could maintain it indefinitely.

Only one thing marred his enjoyment of the sport. Before a race he was allowed very little to eat or drink. This he was forced to accept without understanding. All he knew was that his stomach felt drawn and taut, but the disagreeable feeling vanished as soon as the race was under way. When the whistle blew wings seemed to lift his feet from the ground, and what were hunger and thirst compared with the sweet taste of victory!

In every contest, whether important or not, his will to win made him one with his rider, because the boy loved racing with an intensity that matched his own. With Jumper's strong, fleet legs to carry him the boy for the first time in his life was the equal, and perhaps, the superior of his comrades. Together, the horse and boy liked to believe themselves invincible.

Sensing his small rider's every move and whim, Jumper obeyed the slightest motion of the reins. Held firmly they indicated that he was to conserve his strength. If they slackened he could pick up speed. And if, when the reins were slack and free, the boy struck him lightly with the ends and clapped his legs against his ribs, Jumper knew that he was being urged to give all he had.

Jumper's attachment to the little master was immeasurably strengthened by their common love of racing. Their understanding made them almost one physically: in a race one was incomplete without the other. This bond tended to exclude the master, who was too old for games and pleasures of this kind. Perhaps he was glad to give the care of the colt to his son, whom life had deprived of so many normal boyish activities. At any rate the boy and the colt became partners.

Once they very nearly came to grief, because of their youth and their confidence in each other.

It was shrovetide, and shrovetide in old Russia was a time of merry-making. The entire village turned out for the last festivities before observing Lent. There was singing, the music of bells— the sound of loud, gay voices. Jumper knew that something was the tinkling sleighbells and the great booming church bells—and in the air when overnight he and the other horses were decorated with multicoloured ribbons plaited into their manes and tails, giving them a giddy and festive air. Moreover, his rations had been cut for several days, he had been taken on long walks which plainly had a purpose, and several secret trial races had been held at night.

But when one morning Jumper was given almost nothing to eat and only a couple of mouthfuls of water, the anticipation of something exciting about to happen did not prevent him from complaining. For the master's benefit he pawed the floor, nudged him roughly, and opened his mouth with a long, sonorous 'Hee-ee-ee-aa-a' which was meant to convey his miserable hunger. But the master refused to be moved, and merely watched the stable preparations with a stern and preoccupied air.

When he had exhausted all his tricks and wiles, Jumper thought he saw one last chance. Everyone had left him, and the boy entered his stall. The boy, Jumper very well knew, was soft and inclined to give him anything he wanted. Slyly and with the instinct of an actor, Jumper repeated the performance which had failed to move the master. He reared, bellowed, and flung himself about in such a way that the boy was genuinely alarmed.

In his anxiety to pacify his friend, Denis gave Jumper a little food—a half measure of oats and enough water to wash it down. As he did so he kept a wary eye on the door. Jumper thanked him with a contented 'He-ee-a'. Then both of them dismissed the incident from their minds.

Shortly afterwards the master led Jumper through the village, down a snow-covered road to the starting post. By then the oats and water were making themselves felt, and Jumper was uncontrollably playful. Several times the master was forced to scold him.

'Come now! Enough of this, Jumper. What has got into you? I never knew you to behave so badly.'

But Jumper paid no attention. He was like one intoxicated. His spirits were beyond his control.

At the starting post, with the boy on his back, and a rival colt—a lean bay—beside him, he still refused to obey the reins and line up. Instead he lunged ahead of the signal, or else shied off the road in a most aggravating manner. The master tried to control him, first by being stern, then by cajoling, but Jumper refused to respond. Slanting his eyes at the man he caught a look of perplexity on his face, and the realization that his friend was not sure of him excited him even more. He knew he was making a fool of himself, and his behaviour surprised and bothered him, especially because he was beginning to perspire and to feel a strange heaviness in his legs and body.

After several attempts he finally was pulled into line, the signal was given, and to the accompaniment of shouts and cries the race was on. The familiar din aroused Jumper, and he settled down to the business at hand.

At first he ran nose and nose with the bay. Then, restrained by the boy's touch, he slowed down until he fell half-a-length behind. This was a familiar method of conserving strength. In a little while, when the bay showed signs of weariness, Denis would give Jumper the sign to pick up speed.

So it had been in every other race, and so it would be now. But Jumper's will to run and to win a victory was not enough. He felt himself perspiring strangely, and his stomach was like a dead weight pinning his legs to the ground. His breath came with difficulty; there was not enough air to fill his lungs. Instead of clinging to his rival's side, he began to fall farther and farther back.

Now came the awaited signal. The boy loosened the reins and pressed his ribs, giving him full freedom to go ahead. Then, as Jumper continued to lag, he whacked his perspiring flanks with the leather thongs.

'Gi-up!' Denis urged him. 'Come along now. Give it all you have!' His voice was tense and a little frightened.

Jumper shuddered when he felt the blow. But, obediently, he made a great effort, and for a time ran without losing any more distance. This was the best he could do. There was no strength left in him, and although he continued to run he gradually fell so far behind that he was no longer in the race. His breath came in gasps, his knees sagged, and his eyes could not distinguish anything in front of him.

With his strength went his self-assurance. He didn't expect to overtake the bay—and he didn't much care.

When it seemed that there was not another step left in him, he felt the reins tighten and heard the welcome order to stop.

Covered with sweat and foam, Jumper stood breathing like an engine, submitting with unwonted meekness while his flanks, legs, and mouth were being examined. What was even more surprising: he didn't object even when strangers crowded in around him.

After a while the master took him home, and walked him up and down the yard for a long time. Then he was returned to the stable, and covered snugly with a blanket after his wet body and been rubbed dry. Before leaving, the master fastened his head high, opened his mouth, and emptied in it the bitter contents of a large bottle.

'Yes,' the master said, as if Jumper had asked him a question. 'It wasn't your fault. It was your stupid young friend who fed you oats and water before a race. He was the one who caused you to lose. Forgive him. He thought he was helping you. Ignorance is a dangerous thing. However, several bottles of this stuff will fix you up.'

Jumper swallowed the mixture, confident as ever in the master's judgment, and in a few days his appetite and vigour began to return. The boy, who attended him constantly, watched his progress with mounting happiness. A dozen times he threw his arms around the colt's neck, and touched his muzzle with his lips, murmuring:

'It was all my fault, Jumper. It was all my fault. I'm sorry. But you do forgive me, don't you?'

Jumper nuzzled him playfully, responding instinctively to the gentle sound of the boy's words which he did not understand.

The period of convalescence was pleasant as it gave Jumper a great deal of his friends' company. When it was over the daily outings with the master and boy were resumed. To miss a day was punishment. Without exercise he became restless and was easily excited. At such times the sight of some fillies at a distance was enough to set him wild. For Jumper was now in his third year. He was mature and instinct informed him of Nature's supreme law—that each individual, to complete himself, must pass on life to a new generation.

Chapter 17

Seasonal changes in the weather played an all-important part in Jumper's life. Like every other animal, he reflected the moods of nature. Warmth delighted him, filling him with tireless and boisterous energy. Rain made him languid. Cold caused his body to contract as if in fear of an unseen enemy.

With as much joy as before he greeted one morning the sun of his third summer. Later, in a corral which he occupied alone, he raced the length of the enclosure, circled and returned, snorting with satisfaction, his short mane and thick dark tail streaming in the breeze. Round and round he sped, came to an abrupt halt, and stood rooted, while his ears and eyes strained towards the distant fields, and his nostrils widened, inhaling the gentle air.

The white colt, sluggish as always, paced the adjoining corral. During the winter he had grown and taken on weight, and now he was a huge, broad-chested fellow. Catching sight of Jumper, he ambled with more than his usual show of energy to the fence that separated them. Jumper ran to meet him. But when they came together it was to snort in shrill fury, and to paw the ground into flying bits. Perhaps they accused each other of faithlessness, not understanding the reason for their separation. But more probably the months they had spent apart had dimmed the memory of their friendship, and they met as strangers, each feeling the need to assert his superiority.

'Hee-ee-ee-e!' shrieked Jumper.

'Hee-ee-eee!' the white colt replied rudely.

Up and down the scale their voices ranged as they hurled insults back and forth, until one of the men in the yard could stand their clamour no longer.

'Quiet, you worthless devils!' he shouted. 'Another sound out of you and I'll give you something to shout about.'

They stopped, but in the weeks that followed, though they lived side by side, Jumper and the white colt never became friendly.

This spring Jumper had everything he desired but freedom, and this accounted in part for the ill feeling between him and the white colt. From their enclosures they looked at the open fields and saw other colts enjoying their liberty, and envy made them turn in anger against each other. Especially the sight of passing fillies would throw them into a frenzy of excitement. Then they would race about, neighing madly, and seem on the point of hurdling or crashing a fence. The white colt was much too heavy for jumping, and always, at the last moment, he brought himself up short to place his entire weight against the barrier. Jumper, however time and again rose on his hind legs and tossed his forelegs high, only to lose courage before the final leap. Standing there, pawing the air, he was a picture of dejection. The fence impressed him as much too stout and high for him to cope with.

In bitter longing, his voice rang out across the fields to anyone who would listen: 'Hee-ee-ee-a-a. Can't you see how much I want to be with you?' he was saying. 'Then why don't you do something about it?'

All through spring Jumper was subject to these fits of restlessness. Some mysterious current impelled him towards the others of his kind, promising him fulfilment of an unrealized desire. Yet something always intervened to cheat him of the satisfaction, until one evening he could endure it no longer.

It was dusk. Jumper and the white colt, as usual, were watching the work horses returning from the fields when suddenly their attention was caught by the sight of the piebald filly in a corral only two fences away. In the dim light her graceful body was hardly more than a shadow, but her soft, familiar neigh was enough to excite them intolerably. Tossing their heads in savage impatience, they raced back and forth in their separate pens. When they were tired of running they stood churning the earth with their feet, uttering challenging cries.

Each colt reacted according to his temperament. The white colt, exhausted by the fruitless racing and stamping, contented himself with an occasional snort of protest, as he leaned heavily against the fence, and gazed adoringly at the filly. But Jumper would not give up so easily. It infuriated him that all his efforts to join the filly were thwarted. Time and again, after circling the pen, he charged the fence, rose on his hind legs, and crashed against the bars.

With each failure he became more exasperated. He was determined to have his way. Deliberately, he retreated to the farthermost corner of the corral, stopped, and hesitated for a moment. Then, as he came to a desperate decision, his head went up, the blood of his ancestors asserted itself, and he sped towards the fence. As he came near it, his front legs rose, his hind legs flexed, lifted him, and he was on the other side. Only his hoofs touched the top bar lightly in passing.

The second fence was much lower and presented no problem.

'Hee-ee, hee-ee, hee-ee!' Uttering triumphant whinnies, he ran to the filly and explored her trembling body with his muzzle. Behind his fence the white colt protested loudly at being outwitted, and resumed his frantic pacing.

The filly accepted the attentions with eager but timid interest. Unresisting, she submitted to Jumper's awkward, impassioned caresses. Then quite suddenly the mystery was resolved by an act that left him calm and contented.

When the master and the boy arrived early next morning, Jumper and the filly were standing quietly side by side, as they had stood so many times in the past.

'Eh,' the master said, surprised, 'I don't doubt you've learned another lesson, Jumper—one I couldn't teach you. You are getting to be too clever. Come, let's see what harm you've done.'

Placidly, Jumper followed the old man to the stable, and submitted to a careful examination of his legs. From the tone of the master's voice he understood that he was being reproached for a mad prank.

'To think that you would be foolish enough to jump that fence! It's a wonder you didn't break a leg—and you're not even scratched.'

The boy was jubilant. 'He's a born jumper, Father, don't you think he is? Did you ever know a horse to be so clever? Just wait until I tell the fellows about him!'

Jumper waited patiently until they had finished with him. His eyes did not even stray towards the open door and freedom. A delightful lassitude possessed him, and now and then his flesh quivered as he relived the happy excitement of the preceding night.

Chapter 18

Jumper's childhood was behind him. Little by little he was assuming the responsibilities of a grown horse. Yet he was not done with learning.

With the coming of cooler days the master saddled him frequently and rode him into the forested hills, or the taiga, where he had gone as a young colt with his mother. The dog always accompanied them, making the air ring with his incessant and cheerful barking, and very often the lame boy went along, riding a quiet, lazy, white gelding. On one such trip the five of them remained in the hills for many days.

The gelding was a veteran of the taiga, familiar with the problems of existence in the wild. Wherever they stopped he was given full liberty to graze, but he never strayed beyond the sight and hearing of the master. He was not in the least gun-shy, and he also was wise in the ways of mosquitoes—the most vicious scourge of the taiga. When they had pestered him beyond endurance, he ambled over to the bonfire, which burned day and night, and stood in the direct path of the smoke. There he found relief from his winged enemies.

Jumper was not slow to imitate his companion and to profit by his experience. The more closely he followed the behaviour of the gelding, the more liberty the master allowed him. The rope around his neck was changed to a hobble, and, after a few days, the hobble was removed, and he was permitted to go free.

Jumper looked up to the gelding for guidance, and a sense of companionship developed between them. Everything they did they did together—grazing, drinking at the dancing stream, taking refuge from the troublesome gnats and mosquitoes that worried them. At night they dozed side by side over the smoke from the fire, restful yet ever alert to the innumerable rustling noises about them. If they became separated, the bells they wore around their necks informed each of the other's whereabouts.

Now and then an ominous roar cut through the forest, causing the birds to scatter and the dog's hair to bristle as his tail drooped between his legs, and his bark turned hoarse and furious. What this noise was Jumper did not know. Nevertheless it always set him trembling—not so much from fear as because of the uncertainty, and because it made the gelding tremble.

Almost as terrifying as the roaring sounds were the broad footprints and droppings of some strange animal that they came across occasionally as they grazed. The gelding always halted abruptly, wheeled about with a snort of distaste, and beat a hasty retreat to the camp. Jumper did likewise, though he had no idea why.

He knew something about the wolves, who menaced the herd in the valley, and who, when hungry, even dared approach the village, but he knew nothing of the taiga bears. Because they made their presence known very seldom, and his fright on these rare occasions was soon forgotten, he trusted the taiga with the quiet, protecting shelter of its trees and dense underbrush. With the exception of the gnats and mosquitoes, its inhabitants seemed friendly. The birds who trilled above him and the fuzzy animals that scurried from underfoot and raced along the branches of the trees were not dangerous. As a precaution against surprise attack there was always the dog, who took his duties seriously, setting up a fearful clamour on the least provocation and sniffing for signs of trouble here, there and everywhere.

One night Jumper had his first taste of how deceptive this peace was when a furious storm broke, bringing a beating rain and wind accompanied by flashes of lightning that threatened to split the world in two. Trees swayed dangerously, branches snapped, and solid trunks cracked under the pressure of the screeching wind. To all this, darkness added a mysterious terror.

Jumper was beside himself with fright. Until now he had known danger only as something that had substance and could be seen. But this new enemy that threatened to engulf him, the gelding, the master, the boy and the frantic dog, had no face or body. He would have bolted anywhere to escape it, except that the master held his head, and spoke to him in reassuring tones, as if nothing out of the ordinary were happening.

'There, Jumper, it's pretty bad but I've seen it as bad before. And you will too before you are done.' He kept talking in his soothing sing-song voice. 'We don't have storms as bad as this below—praise God! But there's nothing we can do about it.

You'll learn. God's will be done. If He chooses to strike us—well that's that.'

On and on he droned, now and then interrupted by the boy's childish treble. Jumper's attention was drawn away, so that he hardly noticed when the storm subsided and the fiery blasts that shook his body began to come at less frequent intervals.

At length all was quiet except for the falling rain.

Days passed and they still remained in the taiga. The woods were thinning out as the yellowing leaves fell to the ground, making a thick soft carpet into which Jumper's feet sank with a rustling noise. The nights were getting colder, and the days shorter.

The master and the boy were not the only humans in the taiga now. In nearby clearings other people were camping with their horses, and the voices and neighs rising in the clear sharp air above the meadow had a familiar and comforting sound.

These people were here for a purpose; they were gathering cedar nuts, called 'peasant conversation', which yield a delicious oil as well as meat. The master and the boy went about picking up the strong-smelling cones and flinging them into sacks for Jumper and the gelding to carry back to the camp. Jumper saw with what relish the boy broke them open, extracted the nuts, and cracked them with his teeth. But though Jumper sniffed the cones curiously, he did not find the sharp resinous smell tempting.

More days went by. Other campers returned to their homes in the valley, and still the master lingered, to hunt and also to seek out the nesting places of the squirrels whose pelts would be valuable later in the season. Jumper began to get restless. It was high time that they, too, were home, and he tried by plaintive neighing to convey his impatience to the man.

Although there was an abundance of food, both horses became noticeably thinner. The mountain grass was not as nourishing, and did not tend to produce fat. Jumper, who had an insatiable appetite for bread, missed the delicacies he received at home. The scanty story of stale bread was needed for the master and the boy.

'Whoosh!' the master said, when Jumper nuzzled him inquisitively. 'I've nothing for you. Be off.'

But a few minutes later, behind a tree, Denis would produce from his pocket a crust that was all the more delicious because it was given on the sly.

'Just a tiny piece,' he apologized. 'Father won't miss it if you don't tell.'

With the advance of winter the mosquitoes and gnats disappeared, but this improvement was offset by a scarcity of good grazing. Plagued by constant hunger, Jumper and the gelding got in the habit of wandering away from camp at night, and if they were fortunate enough to find a plot of lush grass they did not return until morning.

It was on one of these foraging expeditions that tragedy struck at them swiftly and without warning.

The two horses had found a particularly fine sheltered spot which as yet had not been touched by the frost. Jumper had wandered a short distance from the gelding, and, raising his head now and then, listened for the bell of his companion. Everything was still, and danger was farthest from his thoughts. Suddenly a pungent odour assailed his nostrils, became stronger, and in a quick, convusive movement his head shot up as he poised his body of flight.

For a second he did not know which way to run: towards camp or towards his companion? His stiffened ears turned this way and that, and his eyes tried to pierce the darkness.

Then out of a thicket near him plunged the gelding. The bell around his neck was jangling furiously, and his laboured breathing indicated his alarm. Close on his heels came a huge, black creature.

Jumper reared, and dashed ahead of the gelding. But just as he turned his companion stumbled over a fallen tree, and the enemy pounced on him with a triumphant roar that filled the woods.

Jumper did not stop. Driven by a terror that obliterated everything else in his mind, he cleared logs and brushed past the outreaching arms of trees which any other time would have blocked his passage. He had only one thought—to reach the safety of the camp, and escape that horror-laden cry.

In camp the boy caught him by the halter and ran a thin hand over his quivering body.

'There, Jumper,' he soothed the colt. 'Take it easy now. Father will get that bear.'

Already the master had snatched the gun and was heading for the thicket, hard on the heels of the dog who was decrying noisily his own lack of watchfulness. In a minute they heard the master's voice in sharp command, followed by an enraged howl from the dog. Then a lumbering movement as of a heavy body crashing through the brush. Then two shots—and silence.

The terrifying night dragged slowly. Jumper kept close to the boy and looked often towards the thicket, expecting to see his comrade. But only the master and the dog returned—the latter spattered with blood and with the air of a conquering hero.

At daylight Jumper went to the stream for water, and, having had his fill, sent a loud neigh summoning the gelding, but only the echo answered. Not satisfied, he left the stream and walked into a thicket beyond which lay the familiar grazing spot. He moved slowly, cautiously, not wholly trusting the silence, and was not unprepared when the same strange, pungent odour assailed his nostrils. For a moment he paused irresolutely, but the desire to find his companion overcame his fear, and he pushed farther into the brush.

A few more steps, and he pulled up sharply with a snort of surprise. There, before him, on a bed of trampled grass and blood, lay the motionless gelding, his throat slashed and with gaping wounds on his neck, flanks, and back. Beside him lay a shaggy, black body with viciously bared teeth.

Rigid with loathing, Jumper gazed for a brief moment, then, wheeling in his tracks, fled headlong back to camp.

Although he stayed close in after this, he still found no peace. Because soon the master appeared with the hides of the gelding and the bear, which he hung between two poles to dry. Their sight and smell were a constant, silent reminder of the tragedy.

A few days later the master saddled Jumper, and was ready for the journey home. Jumper recognized the signs and pawed the earth, impatient to be off. But when the two repulsive hides were tossed on his back he reared in protest. This was more than he had bargained for. The odour of the bearskin was not only nauseating, it was frightening. But the habit of obeying orders conquered fear, and when the boy mounted him the proximity of his trusted friend restored his calm. If the boy was not afraid of the hides, there was no reason why he should be.

'Giddap!' Denis slapped the reins lightly against the colt's side, and they followed the master and the dog along the trail that led to the valley. The dog darted here and there, disappearing into the brush and suddenly reappearing again, always inquisitive and full of his own importance.

It was not until Jumper reached the dear, familiar yard that he again felt at one with the world. The scent of fresh straw, the coming and going of friendly animals, the atmosphere of security and abundance—these were things not to be exchanged for adventure.

Yet was home invariably secure?

Late one night the bell on the village church awoke the entire community. People came rushing from a hundred directions, shouting and waving their hands. All the livestock was hastily assembled and taken from the barnyards to a field on the edge of town. There was screaming and weeping, the wild cries of frightened animals rushing helter-skelter, and the shouts of men giving orders.

Jumper and several other horses were hitched hurriedly to sleighs that were piled high with clothes and household goods. They were led to a safe place, and there they stood until daybreak, while the townspeople battled fierce flames that licked a group of wooden buildings, sending showers of sparks and rolling clouds of smoke towards the heavens.

The unnatural illumination and the acrid smoke that stung his nostrils excited Jumper beyond endurance, and with the other horses he snorted, twisted, and beat a tattoo with his hoofs, as his apprehensive eyes watched the commotion in the distance. Although he understood nothing of what was happening, a sixth sense warned him that here was a ruthless enemy more to be dreaded than the bear: man's and his enemy alike.

With the coming of morning he was returned to his stable, and the accustomed pattern of his life was resumed. The fire had not affected him, because the master's possessions had escaped its greedy tongue. Yet that night left its mark upon him. From that time on he knew the difference between fires: the friendly man-made bonfire that provided warmth and banished insect pests, and the night fire that was not of man's making and that brought terror in its wake.

Chapter 19

No one doubted, least of all Jumper, that he was his master's darling and the favourite of the whole yard. Every motion he made had in it a proud consciousness of his superiority. Whether in rare repose or in action he always succeeded in drawing attention to himself. With the instinct of a showman he could display his grotesquely lean body, his heavy mane, and his showy trumpet of a tail so that they appeared inordinately graceful.

'You see how handsome I am,' his flashing eyes said. 'Surely you cannot resist me.'

But if Jumper was a favourite through a conscious exercise of his charms, he became a hero quite by accident when on a bitter night in January his fleet legs saved the master and the boy from certain death.

That day the master came to the stable early, and hitched Jumper to a light sleigh. Something special was afoot: his Sunday clothes, freshly scrubbed face, and neatly combed beard indicated a holiday outing of some sort.

The master was in gay spirits and sang as he worked on the leather fastenings. When the last buckle was in place the old man called to the boy, who also was dressed in his best, and in high good humour they climbed into the sleigh. Instinctively Jumper responded to the festive mood of his friends, as he carried them swiftly along the hard-packed road to a nearby village which he remembered visiting before. The contented voices and occasional laughter behind him, and the bright, clear sky above, lent strength to his legs. He was completely happy.

But when they arrived in the village Jumper, still hitched to the sleigh, was left standing under a rude shelter. No one came near to speak to him or to bring him food. Every now and then he neighed, demanding attention, but only some neighbouring horses responded half-heartedly. Despite the blanket with which he was covered he was chilled to the bone, and the hunger made him irritable. The aroma of fresh hay and the sound of a horse munching it reached him through a window of a nearby stable. From the street came the sounds of hilarious singing voices, the jangling of tambourines, the trampling of feet, and the screech of sleigh runners on snow.

Jumper had learned that holidays were easily distinguishable from work-days. There was always more noise of a different and happier kind, and very often the master's behaviour underwent a subtle change. He started the day joyously, and the joy apparently spread from his head to his feet, until they began to perform odd and unpredictable antics. On such occasions he was very affectionate and embarrassingly playful. 'You are my true friend, Jumper—my only friend,' he would insist loudly, flinging his arms around the colt's neck. Sometimes he wept, while at other times he amused himself by crawling under the colt's belly and tickling him.

Jumper's mind associated holidays with a foreign odour that mingled with the familiar scent of strong tobacco. He didn't like or understand it, but he had learned to regard it as a warning, and a signal for caution. When the master smelled and acted in this unaccountable manner Jumper had to be patient and cautious.

On this occasion it was quite dark when he at last heard the familiar voices. They were some distance away, but they were coming nearer, accompanied by a large group of strangers.

'Hee-ee-ee-aa-a!' Jumper welcomed them, and pawed the snow to make them hurry.

There was no response except the humming of voices, as a dozen men assisted the master into the sleigh. He sprawled where they had flung him, and shouted unintelligible words. Then Jumper felt the reins grow taut.

'Giddap.'

Obedient as always, in spite of being hungry and neglected, Jumper swung carefully into the road. He knew it was the boy and not the master who held the reins. The hands were not as firm and experienced, and the young voice that reached him above the screech of the runners was affectionate and a little anxious. As Jumper gathered speed a warmth spread through his body, and the pleasant sensation made him forget his hunger.

The night was eerie. Except for an occasional grove of black trees the gently rolling earth was concealed under a covering of snow. A bright moon lighted the scene and cast weird and moving shadows.

Behind Jumper the master's hoarse voice rose in a song. Then the singing stopped, and was followed by snores.

'Faster, Jumper. Hurry home . . . home . . . home,' the boy was saying.

Jumper pricked up his ears. 'Home' was a word he knew well, and, besides, there was an urgent note in the thin voice that conveyed fear. He increased his pace. The road was familiar. Beyond the small woods, now visible in the distance, was a turn and a slight incline. Then nothing but a straight, clear stretch to the village.

They reached the woods, passed through them, and were approaching the turn at the foot of the hill when an ear-splitting howl broke the quiet, and shadowy forms spread fan-wise behind the sleigh. Jumper did not need the boy's terrified cry nor the slap of the reins to start him sprinting at top speed. The hill up which he had to go was neither long nor steep, but it slowed him down, and gave the pursuing pack an advantage. At the crest he was sure that the wolves would close in on him in another second. Their triumphant howls sounded frighteningly near. The shadows took on a definite form, and acquired cruel, fiery pinpoints for eyes, and gaping jaws with lolling tongues.

Straining every muscle, now that the climb was over, Jumper raced down hill along the final stretch of road. The weeping boy frantically told him that the danger was great, and that only he—Jumper—could save them. But this was not what he needed to give him confidence. He needed the master's calm voice and firm grip on the reins.

Try as he would, he could not gain on his pursuers. Several wolves were racing alongside the sleigh, waiting for an opportune moment to attack. Their pungent odour maddened him.

Then, when all hope seemed gone, the howling of the wolves, the anguished cries of the boy, and the swaying of the sleigh finally roused the master. Instantly he grasped the situation and took charge.

'On, Jumper—on, dear fellow. You can do it.'

His voice pleaded, but it was neither excited nor frightened. Jumper, taking new courage, found strength to redouble his efforts.

In the ensuing race everything was a wild confusion. To shake the pursuit the master tossed a blanket out of the sleigh. Several of the wolves attacked it hungrily, and in doing so fell behind.

But one, an enormous beast, refused to be fooled. With great leaps he kept gaining on the sleigh in an effort to reach Jumper's head. He seemed to know that his only hope of stopping them was in getting at the horse.

Closer he came, pounding the firm snow at Jumper's side. A little more, and he would make a lunge. Instinctively Jumper sensed the new danger and pressed forward, his long neck extended, his ears flattened, and every nerve poised for the attack.

'On, Jumper—on!'

The wolf now was aware of Jumper's determination, and with the village only a short distance away he had to take a desperate chance. He lunged, missed, crashed against the shaft, and fell under Jumper's speeding hoofs.

It all happened in a single terrifying moment. Jumper felt the bump and something crunching underfoot, heard the blood-chilling cry of pain, and then the gleeful howl of the pack as they fell on their crushed leader.

They were out of danger, but Jumper did not relax until he was well within the limits of the village. He pulled up at the gate of his own yard. The dog met and greeted him boisterously, and the horses in the stable neighed, welcoming him home.

Only now he realized how deathly tired he was. But before he could enjoy the snug comfort of the stable he had to submit to a thorough rub down. Then the master walked him up and down the yard until his overheated body had resumed its normal temperature.

In the meantime the household came to life, and people gathered around to hear about the adventure, and to pay their respects to the hero.

'Jumper! . . .'

'Jumper, you are a wonder! . . .'

'Jumper, you are the finest horse in all the world! . . .'

Delighted to be the centre of such admiring attention, he longed to prance and to show off, but he was too exhausted. Meekly he accepted the congratulations and affectionate pats, and settled under a warm blanket for the night.

He was content, not because he was a hero but because these people to whom he belonged loved him and in some unaccountable way were pleased.

Chapter 20

Although Jumper was harnessed almost daily that winter, the chores assigned to him were so light that he considered them as recreation rather than labour. The loads of hay, straw, and wood that he was required to pull were no burden at all. In this and in other ways he was shown special favours. Even the stable hands regarded him as one set apart from his companions by certain qualities commanding their affectionate respect. They gave him the simplest tasks, and saved for him the choicest foods.

After the adventure with the wolves his fame spread. Complete strangers asked to have him pointed out to them, and vied with each other in congratulating the master on possessing such a remarkable horse. The story of his exploit passed from mouth to mouth among the villagers, and lost nothing in the telling; a number of embellishments were added for the benefit of visitors.

'That Jumper . . . The huge wolf had him by the throat, and Gerasim was committing his soul to God, when this miracle happened! . . . How can anyone say that a horse has no mind and soul?'

Jumper knew nothing of his growing fame, but he made another important discovery. For the first time he became aware of the women in his master's household. Until then he had accepted them as familiar but unimportant creatures who had no bearing on his comfort and happiness. He was accustomed to obey the men, and he reserved his affection for them.

To find himself suddenly the object of attention from this totally unexpected quarter was surprising and gratifying. The women who came to pet and flatter him often brought him bread dainties, and he tolerated their presence graciously. There was one among them he set apart as worthy of deeper regard. She was a tall, lean, withered woman whose voice and smile were a caress. She visited him usually in the company of the master or the boy—a circumstance which singled her out.

'Ma-ma,' the boy called her.

Jumper had no difficulty in accepting this woman as a friend because some quality she radiated invited his confidence. His animal instinct discerned in her a person of character enriched by experience. When she called him softly: 'Jumper . . . Jumper'—he came readily within reach of her hand. He could never give her the full measure of affection he gave the master and the boy, but he trusted her.

So life went on, in peace and abundance. Then one day, when the sun had gathered strength and had stripped the earth of its white covering, from his corral Jumper saw prancing around the yard a very small colt who struck him as oddly and disturbingly familiar. As he watched the young one play, he became more and more excited. His neck stretched, his nostrils swelled, and his eyes opened wide as he examined the newcomer minutely and tried to identify him. His colour was like his own, he was very graceful, and he carried his tail at an absurdly arrogant angle. No colt he ever had seen had impressed Jumper as much.

He was pondering about it when he heard an anxious 'Hee-ee-ee-a-a', and, shifting his eyes, saw the piebald filly. The sight of her increased his agitation, and his answering neigh was a challenge. But his old playmate did not spare him so much as a glance. She was absorbed entirely by her young charge.

Indifference always angered Jumper. Now he snorted furiously and circled the corral, longing to escape and to join those two who had aroused his curiosity. He had no doubt that he belonged at their side.

After a while Denis and his mother came out, gave him bread, and tried to calm him with kind words. They pointed at the colt.

'Little Jumper,' they said. 'A fine fellow. You should be proud.' And the boy added gleefully, 'You are a papa, Jumper.'

What they said made no sense, but as the days passed, and as he continued to watch the filly and the colt from a distance Jumper's conviction grew that somehow these two were near and dear to him. From time to time he was tempted to imitate the young scamp. Kicking up his heels, he would run and jump as if to say that his own youth was not dead, but these outbursts never lasted long. He was not as light or as graceful as he had been, and the effort soon bored him, especially because his antics attracted no attention.

Then came a day when the young mother looked in his direction and answered his neigh. Jumper was beside himself with joy.

He tore excitedly several times around the corral, pulled up at the fence, and stood quivering.

But his real triumph came several days later, when the master took him to the piebald filly and let them be together again. Afterwards the old man returned, leading a very young and reluctant colt. With a gentle push he placed the creature under Jumper's nose. Jumper recognized the youngster he had seen so often with the filly.

'There,' said the master. 'Look at him. Smell him. He's your son, Jumper, and as fine a colt as you were.'

Even though Jumper did not understand, the closeness of the odd little fellow gazing at him with large, frightened eyes gave him a great deal of pleasure. He sniffed the colt's body contentedly, then, raising his head, sent a triumphant 'Hee-ee-aa-a' across the yard.

Before the sound of Jumper's voice had died, other horses answered him from every direction: 'Hee-aa, hee-aa, hee-aa.' It was as if his friends knew and were extending him their congratulations.

PART III

Chapter 21

The spring and summer of 1914 were exceptional in Zabaikal, and throughout Siberia. Never had the country known such bumper crops. There was rain in abundance, and by July the maturing wheat looked lovely as it strained skyward to meet the rays of the sun—a sea of shimmering green—while the full-eared corn gave promise of a splendid harvest.

The hearts of the peasants swelled with thankfulness as they surveyed the land. A few elders, learned in signs and omens, said gloomily that the unusual number of mushrooms presaged war. But the younger people, ignorant and foolish, laughed at these warnings which were soon forgotten.

Already the hay was raked and stacked, and everywhere peasants were working like beavers. It was not too early to give thought to the long, cold winter ahead, when livestock as well as men must eat. They worked willingly, joyously, as people work who are amply rewarded.

All day long they laboured, from sun-up until sun-down, from Monday until Saturday. But on Sabbath eve, as on the eve of a great holiday, they stopped of one accord to return to the village and enjoy the luxury of a steam bath. Then, with their bodies cleansed of sweat and grime, they were prepared to worship God, and to spent their time in dancing and singing, or simply resting.

Sitting in front of their houses, their souls at peace and their stomachs comfortably full, the elders nodded to passing neighbours and voiced their gratitude: 'This is real weather the Lord has sent us. It's long since we've had a summer like this.'

They had their usual share of grievances. Flies were a cause for bitter complaints. These pests, like the humans, found the weather to their liking, and swarms of them infested the households, getting into post of food and milk, and making the livestock miserable. They seemed determined to make the most of their short life span. The villagers cursed them roundly, and in the same breath excused them with a good-natured shrug of the shoulders.

'Since God gave life to such pests, it is His will,' they said. 'Perhaps there is a reason for them. At any rate, one whiff of cold wind, and they'll be gone for another year.'

The usual misfortunes had to be endured—an occasional death, the burning of a barn, sickness among the livestock. But such incidents as these were not to be escaped, as any man of sense knew. For 'to live a lifetime is something more than just to cross a field,' it was wisely said, 'and no field is smooth all over.'

The villagers of Kubansk had reason to be contented. There was little excitement in their lives, but they did not crave it: they were satisfied to live simply, keep faith with God, and try not to provoke the devil. Their belief in God did not interfere with their belief in ghosts, werewolves, and other good and evil spirits. They accepted them as a part of the scheme of things, which had its own rightful place.

In case you do not know, a werewolf is master of the forest. God forbid that you pass through his domain at night if your conscience is not clear and you have neglected to wear your cross around your neck. For under such circumstances the werewolf takes delight in enticing a man into a thicket so dense that he can never find his way out.

A house-demon is another creature entirely, who as his name implies watches over all domestic creatures. It is said that if he takes a fancy to a horse he will come at night and plait its mane and tail, no matter how often you comb them out. That this is a fact, no Russian peasant doubts. Because Gerasim Ozerov and the boy Denis believed it, they knew that the house-demon loved Jumper. For did they not comb him daily? And did not someone—if not the house-demon, then who?—come in the night and twist the hair back into place? It was a matter of great rejoicing to them that their favourite was so honoured.

Jumper knew nothing and cared less about all this. He was well-fed, well-cared-for, but restless. With every member of the household busy in the fields no one rode or exercised him. Some of his restlessness expressed itself in an open hostility towards the white colt, whose corral adjoined his. The white colt returned the ill-feeling in kind, recognizing in Jumper a rival for the attention of the fillies, but unlike Jumper he found idleness no burden.

The monotony was broken only when the workers did not go out in the fields, and the village temporarily resumed its normal bustling air. One such day Jumper was relishing the knowledge that the master and the boy were home, and that the stables were crowded with work horses. He raced around his corral, stopping now and then to paw the ground and to send a happy 'He-ee-ee-aa-a' of welcome to his friends. To add to the excitement the church bell was ringing, not merrily as it did on holidays, but solemnly. 'Boom! Boom! Boom!' it seemed to say. 'Come and hear my message.'

Obviously, this was not a work day, but the people knew what Jumper could not possibly know: war had been declared, and members of the draft board had arrived in the village to inspect all the horses. Thus, swiftly and unexpectedly, the great outside world was intruding itself on their well-ordered life.

A group of men—villagers and strangers—were making the rounds of the yards, visiting every stable and corral. The visitors were easily distinguishable by their clothes which sparkled and tinkled in a fascinating manner. There was an uproar everywhere they went, as the horses shied away from them, frightened by their dazzling clothes and their rough, crude manner. Even Jumper cautiously held aloof as they came near, although the master was present. Possessed by a strange uneasiness, he would have turned and run had not the master put forward a gentle hand and restrained him.

'There, there, Jumper. Take it easy. Hold on.'

The words were familiar and reassuring, but something was lacking in the master's voice. It was flat and dead, as if someone had drawn a curtain across it to conceal his feelings. Still distrustful, Jumper stood shifting his weight, as the men slapped and poked him. A particularly offensive, fat man with bristling moustaches opened his mouth to peer purposefully inside.

At a sign from the visitors the master removed his bridle. Then before he had time to move, one of the men shouted and, raising an arm, struck his flank with a thin riding crop. Startled by the blow, Jumper shied, as the breath exploded from his nostrils.

The master was alone when he called him to replace the bridle, and Jumper had almost forgotten the blow. He came eagerly and stood beside the master, anticipating caresses and possibly some bread. But the old man was unresponsive and oblivious of the plea in the dark eyes of the horse. Jumper nudged him, as if to say, 'Come, a little attention if you please'—but there was no response.

When the master had adjusted the bridle he suddenly put both arms around the neck of the horse, and laid his face against his glossy coat. 'Jumper . . . Jumper . . .' His muffled voice sounded broken and leaden with grief. An apprehensive shudder ran over the animal's body, and when later the lame boy and the mistress fell on him with similar lamentations, he pricked up his ears in search of an unseen danger.

Almost at once Jumper and a number of other horses, including the white and the chestnut colts, were led from the yard to the village square in front of the church. This was not unusual—Jumper had been there many times before, but now everything seemed to have some deep, dark meaning. He circled, pranced, and turning his head in the direction of his corral, neighed anxiously. 'What is all this about? Where are we being taken? And why are you people standing around making such queer noises and strange faces?'

At the church doors, where he had waited so often for the master and his family, excitement was at its peak. Horses from all the neighbouring farms were gathered there, and among them stood villagers of all ages. The noise, the weeping and exclamations, and the red-eyed faces of the women and children showed that the crowd was under a strong emotional strain.

As he reached the centre of the milling circle, Jumper saw the uniformed visitors who had looked at him only a short while ago. Not too sure of himself, he stood pawing the ground, as one after another the horses were led in front of the strangers. He saw how much time they took with the white colt before dismissing him with an approving slap on his broad quarters. Then the chestnut went forward, and was led away—apparently he, too, met with their approval.

Now it was Jumper's turn. Without hesitation he followed the master to where the visitors stood waiting. But, though the master's touch was as gentle as always, and the comforting aroma of tobacco as overpowering as usual, Jumper stepped warily because the master had a sombre manner, and displayed none of the gay spirits and pride with which he ordinarily showed off his favourite to an audience.

Again the strangers prodded and poked. Resignedly Jumper submitted as they touched his neck, back, and quarters, but when at their request the master walked him back and forth, despite his uneasiness, with so many eyes on him he could not keep from prancing a little. The strangers did not try to conceal their admiration. They gesticulated and exclaimed, and as they became more animated, an increasing gloom settled over the master.

Back in the stable the old man embraced the colt a second time, and again Jumper heard those queer, broken sounds. 'Jumper . . . Jumper. . . .'

In the days that followed life resumed its normal course, and the excitement occasioned by the visit of the strangers was forgotten. From his corral Jumper looked on the same fields and woods, and on the distant, sparkling waters of Lake Baikal. Nothing had changed.

Nothing? . . . He was not sure. Some strange malady had attacked the people around him, and they were given to sudden inexplicable and unheralded outbursts of grief. He had always loved the hours spent with Denis, but though the boy spent entire days with him and showered him with affectionate attentions, now there was a difference which Jumper did not like. The lad's face was so gloomy that the little things they had always enjoyed together were no longer pleasant. Even the bread which Jumper craved as a child craves sweets lost some of its flavour when it was not accompanied by a smile.

'Oh, Jumper,' Denis wailed one day, planting a kiss on the soft tip of his nose. 'Don't you understand? The Czar is taking you away to fight the war, and we'll never, never see you again.'

The kiss had tickled, and Jumper shook his head gravely as he switched his tail, which the boy had just finished combing. It was all very disturbing because he knew that the people he loved were trying to convey some information to him. He did not know what it was, but their unhappiness made him nervous, and he turned for consolation to the chestnut gelding.

For some reason that Jumper did not seek to fathom, his one-time enemy had been relieved of field work, and occupied a corral adjoining his. This was very pleasant, because now that jealousy did not mar their relationship, they found much comfort in being together.

Jumper saw no immediate threat to his comfort and security, when, without further warning, a morning came that changed everything. Jumper, the white colt, and the chestnut gelding were led from their stables into the yard. They expected to be taken to their corrals, but instead heavy ropes were placed around their necks, and Jumper and the chestnut were tied to the rear of a cart, while the white colt was tied to another. This unusual procedure was accompanied by distressing noises from members of the family who had left the house and stood in an excited knot by the gate.

When the signal was given to start Jumper obediently followed the cart, but he was stopped by a shout from Denis: 'Jumper . . . Jumper. . . .' He could not distinguish the other words, but they confirmed a deep-seated suspicion that all was not well. Bracing his body firmly, he halted the progress of the cart, and twisted and turned in a fever of anxiety until the hateful rope threatened to choke him. He would not move another step until the master's gentle words cajoled and reassured him.

At the gate he turned for a last look at the yard. There were his old companions—the enormous figure of his mother and beside her the piebald mare with her dark colt—all standing with their ears pointed curiously as they watched the departing caravan. He longed to be with them but the rope left him no choice. At the turn of the road when the farm and its inhabitants were lost from view, as a final protest he put all his heart in an anguished 'Hee-ee-aa-a', which instantly brought a response but did not dispel his fears.

The very air seemed charged with uneasiness as the carts with horses trailing behind them passed through the village. Other carts joined those of Gerasim Ozerov, and along every street people stopped or came out of their houses to watch the caravan drive by. Many young people ran out into the road, and with agonized cries threw themselves on their pets. These wild outbursts were a torture to Jumper's nerves; he shuddered whenever the crowd closed in, and frantically sought some means of escape.

Suddenly, they were beyond the village limits, and in the open country where the sun poured its warm rays on nature at peace. Calm settled on the company, as they moved more confidently at a good clip. Only Jumper seemed to doubt the purpose of the journey. Every now and then he turned his head in the direction of the village and sent a long, resonant neigh of farewell.

Behind the row of carts and horses the dust whirled, rose, and settled its oppressive weight on the flowers and grass by the roadside.

Chapter 22

Once out of sight of home Jumper grew calm and settled to a steady jog. The master was in front of him, near enough to reach out a caressing hand from time to time and touch his muzzle, the fields that unrolled on either side were familiar, and the chestnut by his indifferent manner implied that nothing untoward was happening. There was not after all, he decided, cause for alarm.

Then as hours passed and night and day and another night went by, a great weariness settled over him. It was part physical tiredness and part boredom. For there was nothing to look forward to but a brief stop occasionally to drink at a stream, with time perhaps to nod for a few minutes and exchange neighs with the other horses in the shade of some trees. Such routine was as deadening to the spirit as to the body and Jumper's customary playfulness gave way to stoic indifference.

He had accepted the idea that he would for ever more jog quietly behind his cart when suddenly he discovered to the right and left of him monstrous brick buildings that bore no resemblance to the village houses he knew. Underneath was a hard-surfaced road that reverberated with the thud of many hoofs. And noise and bustle filled the air with excitement. The train of carts had reached the city of Irkutsk, and the change acted on Jumper like a tonic. Now he picked up his legs more smartly, he carried his head high and his eyes rolled from side to side in an effort not to miss any of the wonders about him. Wanting someone to share his pleasure in the strange sights and sounds he deliberately nudged the chestnut gelding, but the gelding refused to be aroused. His dull, sidelong glance said: 'Why get excited, brother? There's nothing here to cause us to rejoice.'

When the caravan came to a halt in a great square Jumper gazed wonderingly at the large assembly. In addition to hundreds of horses and their drivers there were men in bright uniforms with glittering decorations and, helping them, other men more simply dressed who resembled the village peasants except that they lacked beards. The uniformed men, whose brilliance frightened the horses, went from cart to cart inspecting the animals and singling out one or another. Whenever they gave a signal the attendants led away the chosen horses to a fenced enclosure.

Watching several of his companions disappear in this manner, Jumper grew uneasy and whinnied plaintively as he danced at the end of his rope. The master came over to him.

'Quiet, Jumper,' he said. 'You don't like this, I know. Neither do I. It's a bad business. But who are we to tell the government what to do? You'll make a good soldier!'

The master's voice, while soothing, was not cheerful and Jumper continued to eye the proceedings doubtfully. When a big man with a fierce moustache approached, took the rope from the master, and pulled him in the direction of the fence, he was thoroughly frightened. With a toss of his head he tore himself free and returned to the cart. But the strange man would not leave him. He and another man followed, again grabbed the rope and, swinging the free end threateningly, pulled with greater determination than ever.

Though Jumper reared, lunged, and whinnied a terrified appeal to the master, he was helpless. The stinging lashes of a whip, intended to subdue him, only frightened him the more and set him to pawing the air in a frenzy. But he could not escape the tug of the rope and the men's threatening cries. At last, resigned, he followed his tormentors, but stopped at the gate of the enclosure to throw a last backward glance at the cart which now seemed to him a haven of security.

The master was standing as he had left him, his arms raised in the air. He called something, but Jumper understood only two words '. . . Jumper . . . Jumper.'

With a loud neigh Jumper reared again, but this brought only another shower of blows. Quivering with terror, he went through the gate and when he next looked behind him the master was lost from sight.

As he was being tied to a post a familiar neigh close by made him turn his head. There was the chestnut gelding, as comfortably stolid as always. His presence was reassuring but did not wholly dispel Jumper's fears. He continued to look about him with mistrust at the bustling men who wore clothes the colour of autumn grass, and who filled the air with their shouts and imprecations.

Jumper did not know that the men were as unfortunate as he.

Most of them were peasants, torn from their loved ones, and put in uniforms. They were not angry with him, as he supposed, but at the circumstances which drove them to perform unpleasant duties. And one of the duties they liked least was depriving other peasants of their mainstays—their horses.

With Jumper's arrival at the Fifth Horse Mobilization Centre he entered a world completely foreign to the one he had known. The wide-open yard with its posts and the high fence painted brown was the first step of his military career. The strangeness of the place made a deep impression on Jumper. There was nothing about it to remind him of the pleasant village yard. He did not understand that he was destined to become a soldier.

Chapter 23

A civillian is not transformed into a soldier overnight, and a barrack is never a home. From the moment he entered the dreary enclosure Jumper felt the difference. The master's stable was not a palace, but at least it offered snug protection from the weather, and the people had been kind. Here there was neither protection nor kindness.

For the first time Jumper knew what it was like to be afraid of human beings. All day long he stood in front of an empty crib, tied by a short rope to a post. From time to time someone threw an armful of mouldy hay into the crib. He would have scorned to touch such stuff in the master's yard, but here he ate it greedily. When he finished he even searched the ground for wisps that might have dropped, but he moved furtively, in order not to attract the attention of the uniformed men, whose likes and dislikes were inexplicable. They seemed to begrudge him food as well as liberty. They gave him nothing to do, and yet on the slightest provocation they lashed him cruelly. And, most confusing of all, the people looked alike. Though some were gentler than others, he could not tell them apart. A soldier had only to approach and his whole body began to quiver in anticipation of ill-treatment.

Thirst was a greater enemy than hunger, but men were worst of all. He welcomed the nights when no one came to harass him, and when there was relief from the parching sun.

It was a consolation to have the chestnut and the white colt not far away. All rancour was dead in him, and even the white colt seemed a link with happier days. The hundreds of strange horses all around did not interest him. On his arrival curiosity had tempted him to inspect his neighbours, and especially to attract the attention of a black mare who was tethered nearby. But soon his misery began to occupy him to the exclusion of everything else: he had no thought but to relieve his hunger and thirst, and to avoid the angry men.

Desolate days dragged on. Every morning Jumper looked for something to release him from the repulsive yard, but nothing happened. A stiffness settled in his legs, and he tried to relieve it by shifting his weight, but this did not help. Then, following the example of the chestnut, he tried to lie down. This afforded temporary relief, but in the end it only added to his misery, because the short rope pulled his neck, and heavy rains had mixed the dirt and manure into a thick mass which caked on his body and made it itch unbearably.

No other torment seemed possible, but there was something else: an excruciating pain in the tender muscles of the fetlocks, brought on by constant immersion in the mud. His legs always before had known the luxury of dry straw, and were soft. Between the pain and the itching he was miserable and extremely nervous.

A fury of restlessness, pain and hunger at intervals drove Jumper to gnaw the wooden post to which he was tied. He saw other horses resorting to this practice, but beyond providing an outlet for his temper, it brought little relief. The wood was hard, ill-smelling, and tasteless. Now and then, from sheer weariness, he closed his eyes, and when the world around him became obliterated, he seemed to recreate vague images out of the past. They were like bits of an improbable dream: an old man whose very presence was an assurance of comfort . . . a limping boy, his face smiling, and his hand extended in a caress . . . and all around green peace, sweet-smelling quiet, orderliness and warmth.

Out of habit he raised his head occasionally, and called into the distance: 'Hee-ee-ee-aa.' From all sides horses answered, but the sound lacked vigour and joy. It was more like a plea for compassion. Having been robbed of their security and comfort, these animals were broken, and waited for something they did not understand. They became indifferent, did not bother even to turn their heads.

Then, inexplicably, one day everything changed. The thing Jumper had hoped for came to pass. It was a lovely morning—mild and charged with the gaiety of spring. The yard became filled with men in grey, all shouting and making a terrific noise. One by one the horses were untied and led into the middle of the yard, where a group of men in uniforms waited, their voices raised in command.

Jumper did not know that these strange men were members of

a military commission assigned to inspect the yard; that they were appalled by the conditions they found, by the sick and half-starved horses, and by the mud and filth. He did not know that the furious exclamations were directed not at the horses but at the stupid, greedy men in charge of them. What interested Jumper was that here at last was an opportunity to walk some of the stiffness out of his joints. At first the slightest movement was painful, and his knees refused to bend. But by stepping unnaturally high and shaking each leg before setting it gingerly on the ground, he soon felt a resurgence of life.

Back and forth he paced across the yard, slowing or quickening his step in obedience to shouted directions. Everything that was required of him he was willing to do with a growing sense of pleasure because it was apparent that the strangers were sympathetic and had no thought of using a whip. Gentle hands felt his body. One bearded fellow who had been especially attentive approached and rubbed salve on the tender, itching surface around his fetlocks. The salve burned at first and seemed to aggravate the itching, but soon he felt a distinct relief.

What a day of surprises it was!—not for Jumper alone but for all the horses. After the unaccustomed exercise each animal was allowed to drink his fill of good clean water and—marvel of marvels—given oats and a large armful of sweet-smelling hay. Men even came with currycombs to brush their poor, neglected hides.

Whatever the reason for the sudden change, it was welcome. Jumper felt that once again he was enjoying the comforts of the master's yard. And such was his nature that he very soon forgot his unpleasant experiences. Cheerfully, he expressed his satisfaction with the world by exchanging neighs with his acquaintances. He was no longer indifferent to the attractions of the black mare, and pranced playfully whenever she came near. He no longer shied when the attendants approached, though he watched them warily, not quite ready to give them his full confidence despite their friendliness.

Food, drink, exercise, dry straw, and pleasant if not affectionate treatment at the hands of men. Life once more was desirable, and every day a fresh miracle.

Jumper was interested, but not terrified, when one day all the horses were assembled for inspection, and then driven in groups along the noisy streets through which they had entered the yard.

He went calmly, not disposed to question anything so long as the chestnut gelding was beside him. Between these two former enemies a strong bond had grown. The chestnut, thinner now, was as placid and phlegmatic as ever. They were so engrossed in each other that they came to the end of their journey without realizing it. Suddenly they became conscious of exitement among the other horses. Looking for the cause of it, they saw great roaring, puffing monsters dragging rows of odd-shaped houses.

Jumper pricked up his ears and rolled his eyes. The thing didn't make sense! He stared at the monsters belching black smoke, he heard the shouting of people and the sounds made by frightened animals, and he saw the wildly pleading eyes of horses peering out of the houses on wheels.

In Jumper's village there had been no railway to prepare him for this strange sight. He could not stay calm as one struggling horse after another was led away. He saw the white colt go. Then it was the chestnut's turn.

This was more than Jumper could bear. In blind terror he reared to his full height and strained frantically to follow his friend. He could not free himself, but soon two men came and untied him. With a bound he made after the chestnut, and charged up the runway into the car. The men had no choice but to follow as quickly as they could. Then for what seemed a long time Jumper stood quivering with excitement and fear, and pressed closely against his old comrade. He calmed down only when the men disappeared, and he felt sure that it was not their intention to separate him from the chestnut. For the moment all the horses wanted was to be together.

Later curiosity returned, and Jumper examined his surroundings. This was a strange stable, but there was no reason to complain: underneath was fresh straw, men brought water and nose-bags filled with oats, and when he had finished there was sweet hay to munch. He was aware of the chestnut crowding his shoulder, and the friendly pressure was reassuring.

That night as the horses stood drowsing in the soft air redolent of the country stable yards they had left, the train shrieked, jolted, and settled into a swaying, creaking motion. Jumper held his head upright, prepared to meet a new disaster, but except for the clanging underfoot nothing untoward seemed to happen. He caught the chestnut's eyes questioning him anxiously, and neighed a soft reply.

'Don't be afraid, old friend. This isn't at all bad. There's plenty to eat, it's dry—and we're together. Cheer up!'

As the train gathered speed, the rhythmic motion became soothing. The horses dozed or munched hay, accepting this new turn in their fortunes. They were learning that life—good or bad—must be taken as it comes, and at the moment it was not too bad.

Chapter 24

Stop!—start!—bump!—rattle! Jumper's strange new stable moved, swaying and creaking, to an unknown destination. Day and night followed each other in weary succession until restlessness took hold of the horses as they saw the world in constant motion, and as painful stiffness settled in their muscles, making them irritable.

Along with his travelling companions, Jumper lunged this way and that in the cramped quarters, beat the floor with his hoofs and sent wild cries begging to be released, but to no avail. The men who brought food and water had no patience with such display of emotion. 'Hey, you devils, have you gone mad from good living?' they shouted. 'Pipe down if you don't want a taste of the whip!'

These men were for the most part exactly alike—in their dress, as well as in their manners. Jumper soon learned that it was wise to avoid attracting their attention. They had nothing in common with the villagers among whom he had grown up, who treated animals with understanding and affection. One among them seemed different from the rest. Perhaps it was the man's heavy, greying beard that reminded Jumper of the master and prompted him, when he first saw the stranger, to whinny a greeting and stretch trustingly in expectation of a caress.

Jumper soon realized his mistake. The man seized a broom that was near at hand, and in a fury brought it down on the animal's head. Thereafter Jumper, like the other horses, shied away when the man came near. Only the chestnut had courage to manifest the hatred the others felt. The detested stranger knew this, and had the sense to keep at a safe distance from the gelding, though he had no opportunity to strike him.

The battle between the horse and the man went on day after day. Then, very suddenly, the animals were relieved of the hated man's presence. It happened very simply. He came one evening in a particularly ugly mood, and as usual vented his anger on the chestnut. The gelding accepted the challenge, bared his teeth, and lunged. The man took a hasty step backward and disappeared through the door of the car, to be seen no more.

It was incomprehensible to Jumper, but it was such a minor incident in his new life that even the memory of the man vanished with him.

Other men came, and went. Jumper regarded them all with equal indifference, but gradually, without realizing it, he singled out one man who took on importance. His arrival morning and evening on inspection rounds caused no flurry of nervousness among the horses. Instead, he moved among them as an old acquaintance, addressing pleasant words to them.

One day, to Jumper's complete amazement, he heard the man repeat his name, again and again.

'Jumper . . . Jumper. . . .'

Impulsively Jumper stretched out his neck and was rewarded with a caress. After that he waited impatiently for the man's arrival. He had no way of knowing that the man was a top-sergeant detailed to the horse train, and that it was his responsibility to deliver his charges to a certain artillery regiment stationed in Kiev. As a matter of routine he had been supplied with documents listing all the horses by name. Prompted by a whim, or by boredom, or by some strange fancy, he purchased a notebook and wrote in a clear bold hand on the cover:

'Personal Service Record of the Siberian colt "Jumper".'

On the first page was a neatly inscribed legend:

'To anyone who may find this book, be it known that it is the service record of Jumper, a very gentle horse. I beg anyone into whose hands the horse and this notebook may fall to continue the record of his experiences in the service of our country. In all my life I have never seen a horse with eyes so full of wisdom. They are almost human. I should like to own such a colt for breeding, but I fear that an unhappy fate awaits him, along with most of us. He is no less a soldier than the men. And what can we hope for except death in some engagement? I feel a great pity for him. He resembles none of the other horses, either in behaviour or intelligence.'

Like Jumper, the top-sergeant was a typical product of the Russian village. To him animals were a necessary part of life, and finding this colt who seemed so clearly to understand his ways awakened in him a deep nostalgia for his home. At regular intervals he made notations in his little book:

'Every time I go near the car where Jumper is, he welcomes me with a whinny, and usually before I have had time to speak to him. The other horses are suspicious of me, but not so Jumper...'

'It is good that I have found this friend. I tell him the usual nonsense a man tells a horse, and I could swear he understands every word I say. Whether he does nor not, he is a very attentive listener. . . .'

'I wonder what the other horses make of my conversations with Jumper! "Are you lonely?" I ask him. I am sure he knows how lonely one can be in a crowd. "Do you know what it is to be a soldier? Would horses, if they were to rule the world instead of men, fight monstrous wars?' Jumper nuzzles me, and his eyes say: "I believe everything you believe." Who knows? In any case it comforts me to talk to him.'

Interspersed with these notes were reflections on the war, on the dismal state of the world, and on the relations between men and animals. The top-sergeant was something of a philosopher with a taste for putting his thoughts on paper.

Between his friend's visits, Jumper became more and more impatient of confinement. He was adequately fed and watered but except for brief moments of exercise he had no way of using his stored-up energy. He tried to convey his impatience to the chestnut gelding, but that lazy fellow was not easily aroused. His placid glance seemed to say:

'Why get excited, brother? No good will come of it. Take it easy. Eat, drink, keep your health, and accept life as it comes. We don't know what's ahead, and we would do well to arm ourselves with patience. . . . That is my way of looking at things. . . .'

Whether or not Jumper accepted this simple wisdom, the mere presence of his old friend served to calm him and to make the passage of time tolerable.

Chapter 25

The grey of morning and the spring fragrance of awakening fields entered the half-opened windows and filled the stables. Outside, the manor-house loomed fantastically, a grotesque structure of columns and glass terraces, balconies and fancy cornices, guarded by the smaller buildings which surrounded it. Bordering the estate was a park and beyond the park a river which ran in a shining ribbon and proudly bore on its bank a village with two churches. The silence before dawn had cast its spell, yet there could be felt the stirring life of a new day, soon to be heralded by a myriad of sounds.

As soon as the cocks began to crow Jumper scrambled to his feet from the litter warmed by his body, stretched himself, and pranced the length of the stable to limber his muscles. That rite completed, he thrust his head into the manger, dreamily munched some hay, then, as if to announce that he was awake, he neighed sonorously. The neigh soared through the stable window to blend with the answering 'hee-ee-a's' of other horses and the joyous barking of dogs. Something in the sounds made Jumper stand rigidly at attention, ears cocked, nostrils dilated.

After a winter spent in this comfortable, roomy stable, which did not rock or screech, Jumper seemed to return to his past. Everything reminded him of the village life so dear to his heart—a life in which yesterday, today, and tomorrow were exactly alike, peaceful and yet crowded with activity.

Restlessly he paced the stable and waited for the slightest sound that would announce the arrival of the bearded soldier. Every morning for months had begun with the appearance of this kindly man in grey uniform who was so much like the old master. 'Ah!' was his customary greeting. 'So you are up already. Did you have a good rest? . . .' On and on he talked as he brought water and oats, and then settled to the business of giving Jumper's glossy flanks a good brushing with sure, swift strokes of the currycomb. Jumper loved this morning rubdown and for the most part stood quietly while the man worked. But now and then he squinted his eyes to watch the proceedings, or if the man's head came near he reached out with his lips, snatched the cap from his head, and tossed it in the air.

Jumper felt a great affection for this soldier, who was a vital link connecting him with the more important people in his new life. The soldier and the lieutenant he served had given Jumper the thing he needed most: a master whom he obeyed willingly and without questioning. Without a personal tie with the world of human beings, he was lost.

When the soldier finished his chores this morning would he take down the saddle? Would the master appear, and would they ride out to drill? All winter, as regular as clockwork, the lieutenant had appeared, and they had gone off to take part in an exciting game with many other men and horses. But the last week—since spring had touched the air—had been different. No one had ridden him. He had languished in the stable. Why?

And where was the mistress? She was as much a part of this pleasant existence as the master and the bearded soldier. Each morning, as he stood saddled and waiting for the master, she came out and spoke to him with laughter in her voice, while she proffered him a large piece of bread sprinkled with salt. The bread and the petting he took for granted, looking forward to them with the impatience of a spoiled lover. As for the gracious woman, he accepted her as someone close to the master, and who for that reason alone was entitled to his affection. Yet he never presumed. He could tease the bearded soldier by snatching at his cap, or play with the master, but he never took liberties with the mistress. Towards her he always behaved deferentially, as if he feared that his rough tenderness would offend her.

Jumper had entered fully into the ways of these people, and he found serving them a pleasure. He would not have changed places with anyone. A happy accident had made him the personal mount of Lieutenant Radov of the 234th Siberian Artillery Regiment. Married on the eve of the war, and waiting daily for front line duty, the Lieutenant and his bride lived in the constant shadow of separation, but Jumper in his blind contentment did not know this. In common with children and other animals he assumed that his own satisfaction reflected the state of the world.

Lieutenant Radov had the notebook containing Jumper's service record which the kind top-sergeant had begun. From time to time he made an additional entry, and it gave him much pleasure to see the record grow, because he appreciated the excellent qualities of his horse and was deeply attached to him.

Jumper, the notebook made clear, had in him the stuff of which fine soldiers are made. He submitted readily to military discipline, perhaps because from his earliest youth he had looked up to men and had obeyed their will. He found no difficulty whatever in mastering the details of military formations. Indeed there was something exhilarating in the massed drill with other men and horses—a pleasant excitement reminiscent of the feeling he had experienced at village races long ago. He fretted when the new master, for one reason or another, absented himself from the drills, as he had during the past week.

That night, many months ago, when he and the other horses were taken out of the moving stables and led through the busy, lighted streets of a Russian city, Jumper was ready for the worst. His instinctive fear of new surroundings, however, proved groundless. Fate unexpectedly rewarded him with a kind master, a mistress, and a bearded soldier, to all of whom he quickly became attached. At first he was lonely. He didn't like to be separated from the other horses, especially from his friend the chestnut. But this feeling did not last long. He simply had no time for it because from morning until late at night he was under saddle, taking part in strange and exciting activities that required constant alertness and exacting obedience, not only to his master, but to some will that was felt rather than seen. Sometimes he bore his master at a gallop alongside rumbling iron carts which were drawn by teams of horses; or else he waited while the carts were halted suddenly and strange shining objects belched smoke and fire to the accompaniment of a terrific roar. At first the noise made by the guns caused him to shudder uncontrollably—it was so much louder than the firing by the old master to which he was accustomed—but soon he began to accept it as a matter of course. Without reasoning he understood that these men, horses and strange objects were doing together something that was necessary. He saw no harm in it to himself or to others. And no longer afraid, he was intoxicated by the noise and general excitement which seized him with a desire to run or to gallop like mad. Music also had its magic effect on him—he loved it.

In the evenings when he and the master were returning home, there was almost always music. He didn't know why it made him fling his legs out gracefully, as if he were dancing; he held his head high, and, oblivious of the tired muscles, responded with his entire well-groomed body.

Although he missed his own kind, during the drills hc had the satisfaction of seeing the chestnut gelding, and of exchanging neighs with him. Jumper was one of the lucky horses. He did not have to drag heavy loads, like the others; he was never worked to exhaustion; no one ever struck or shouted at him.

He gathered from the chestnut's neighing that his friend's life was not an easy one. 'Jumper!' his plaintive cries seemed to say. 'You are a lucky fellow. You have only one master, but look at me. I have so many I don't know whom to obey. As for these horrible things with the awful roar that I drag, they are getting on my nerves. I would prefer to pull peasant carts and to plough and harrow the rest of my life rather than be tied to these devilish contraptions.'

Jumper neighed in reply and tried to be sympathetic: 'It is true my life is easy, Chestnut, but you must admit that you don't go hungry, and you're always surrounded by other horses. That's more than can be said for me. Of course, it's not as nice here as it was at home, but it is fun when the shooting begins, or when the music plays.'

The chestnut was not impressed: 'Music! Shooting! Who wants it? No, I prefer the village life with its sensible labour to this useless turmoil. You, Jumper, seem to be getting lightheaded. Don't you realize that we are being made ready for something that will freeze the blood in your veins? Don't you see that these devilish guns shatter trees and make deep pits in the ground? Why? I ask you. Is this what life is for?'

Jumper could sense the unhappiness in the chestnut's neighing, but he was not concerned about the future. He loved to feel the master on his back and himself a part of the exciting life around him. After several months, he learned everything he had to know about drills. He understood the bugle calls which told him when to rise in the morning, when to gallop, when to stop, and when to rest. He understood that grim-looking objects like powder-carts and guns were a necessity, and not to be shied at. Best of all he understood his good fortune in having his master, his mistress, and the bearded soldier to pamper and care for him.

When he was in good humour, the master talked to Jumper as if he were human, or teased him as if he were a child. Not more than a week ago the master had said: 'Jumper, you are being spoiled, and by my own wife! I do believe you like her better than you like me, you beggar!'

At that moment Jumper had been picking daintily bits of bread from the woman's slender, outstretched hand, and he acknowledged the remark only with a toss of his head. The woman had laughed, and had responded with a joke.

But recently there had been other mornings, when the master did not speak and the mistress proffered him bread in silence, when the man and woman had no caresses to spare him, when they spoke to one another in low, anxious tones, and his angry stamping failed to draw their attention. At first he was merely annoyed by this apparent neglect, but when the same thing happened for two or three mornings in a row, annoyance gave way to a vague alarm. Something threatened to disrupt his newly found happiness.

It was later than usual this morning when the tread of boots and a familiar cough told Jumper that this friend, the bearded soldier, was there. He turned his head towards the door and neighed impatiently, as much as to say: 'Well, it's about time!' But when the door opened and the familiar grey-clad figure appeared, he went forward gladly, anticipating a few minutes of play before the serious business of the day began.

But the soldier was not in a playful mood. He reached out his hand to caress the horse's sleek neck, and he spoke kindly, but his face and voice were glum.

'You fine beast,' he grumbled. 'You are glad that I am here, but you don't know the bad news I bring. Today we're going to follow the others—to the front, brother—the master, you and I. Rightfully, we should be going out into the fields to plough and sow. But instead we're going into battle, to suffer and perhaps to die. Jumper, there's a bad life ahead of us!'

The soldier was so affected by his own words that, embracing Jumper around the neck, he began to sob and blow his nose.

Jumper stood motionless. The sound of weeping agitated him, forced him to recall something out of the past . . . that day the soldiers came and took him away from the old master's farm, while the family stood wailing at the gate. . . . But it was only for a brief moment—a moment in which man and animal were brought close together by a sense of common misfortune. Then Jumper was taken into the yard where he capered at the hitching post, as with loud neighs he greeted all his acquaintances within hearing distance. When the chorus answered, he was surprised to discover how many familiar voices were missing. Again and again he called and the woods echoed his 'Hee-ee-ee-aa', which asked that this world remain as it was.

Chapter 26

Night was settling on the hills and forests like a heavy mist, imparting to them fantastic outlines—dark and mysterious. Sparks flared and tongues of flame split the dusk and left a dense, fetid smoke hanging in the air. The sporadic rumble and roar of artillery was punctuated by the chattering of machine-guns and by an occasional report of a rifle that was like the snap of a whip.

For the past week a fierce battle had been raging for the possession of several mountain positions. The peace of centuries was shattered as the majestic Galician hills witnessed a drama of human vengeance and hate. In a few days the very earth seemed to have changed. Smoke and fire had scorched and blackened it until people, animals and birds found life there impossible. But if the inhabitants were miserable and distraught, so were the invaders. Everything was chaos. Carts, wagons, and ammunition cases were scattered everywhere among the bushes, and the defiles were strewn with the still, broken bodies of horses and men. The air was hideous with the cries of the wounded, which momentarily drowned the sound of guns. In the midst of this suffering and death men and horses welcomed darkness as a temporary respite. They knew that the eyes of the enemy were watching from the dark hollows, that night with its comparative quiet was not to be trusted, and that at best it was only a prelude to further horrors. Still it was better than daytime, when even a pretence of safety was impossible.

Jumper, too, welcomed the gathering darkness. Standing beside an empty artillery cart at the base of a great cliff, he was centring all his attention on his neighbour, the chestnut gelding. Around them were other horses, but these two were completely oblivious of them. With their eyes and with an occasional pressure of their bodies the friends imparted to one another their fleeting satisfaction and fears. 'Well,' they could have been saying, 'this was a day! What madness! When will it all end?' They were hungry, tired, and tortured by thirst. But it was one of the advantages of night that soon someone would come and lead them into the valley where a merry stream would refresh them, and where they could crop the remnants of the trampled grass.

Jumper and the chestnut bore only a faint resemblance to the vigorous, well-nourished animals that had started on the campaign. They had shrunk and become smaller, their coats were coarse and without lustre, the skin was drawn tight over the protruding ribs and quarters; their heads hung low. The old jauntiness was gone, having given way to a meek resignation. They endured what they had to endure—battle with its horrible din and smell of death, exhausting marches and the equally exhausting waits. Experience had dulled in them all sense of fear; surrounded by terror, they lived each day on an instinctive knowledge that night would bring a measure of peace. Jumper had long ago lost all sense of time and place; he lost, too, the joy and anticipation each new day had brought. Instead, through sharing hardships and suffering, he had acquired an understanding of his master. This feeling of kinship with a human being was something the chestnut lacked. He had never had a master of his own, and from the time he was taken from the village he had expected nothing good of men. This was not the case with Jumper.

Training had taught him to be calm no matter what happened, even when the hell of battle broke loose around him, but it could not prevent him from being nervous when the master left him. Like a soldier ready for any emergency, he carried the saddle until night when the master relieved him of the burden, wiped away the sweat and comforted him with words and caresses. Only the other night he had said:

'You've grown thin, Jumper. War is a terrible business! Hunger, hunger, and never any peace. Be patient! We're serving our country now, and that means sacrifices. Yet the war cannot last forever. Peace will come, and we will return home and forget. . . . That is, if we return at all. Who knows? You are lucky that God endowed you with the fine instincts of loyalty, obedience and devotion, and spared you understanding of the madness that surrounds us.'

Instinctively Jumper reached for the master, and thrust a moist nose in his face. His great dark eyes seemed to reply: 'Well, no doubt things could be worse. You and I, Master, are not the kind that scare easily. But I am very hungry. Couldn't I possibly have a little something to eat?'

The master understood but was powerless to help. It was the bearded soldier who brought from somewhere a small quantity of yellowed grass and a mouthful of hay.

In the recent months Jumper had learned to value and fight for his meagre fare. If another horse merely looked in his direction, he pressed back his ears and bared his teeth. How dare they covet what belonged to him, even if it was only a miserable, withered branch. Hunger was teaching him avarice and encouraging the instinct of ownership.

The fact that Jumper had become accustomed to the horrors of war—to the ear-splitting noise of rifle and cannon fire, to the sight and smell of violent death—did not mean that he had grown brave, or knew the meaning of bravery. Rather, he had sharpened his instinct for detecting danger before its presence was apparent to human senses. His ears were so acute that he could distinguish between friendly and enemy gunfire; his nose informed him of the proximity of foreign men and horses; his eyes were never deceived by darkness; his legs, accustomed to the uncertainties of the Siberian taiga, took him unerringly where he wanted to go, day or night.

The master and other men learned to value these qualities in him, especially after a certain incident. It had been a day like any other day in Jumper's military life. So he looked in amazement at the soldiers who gathered around him with lavish caresses and kind words. Attention always delighted him, but this occasion was made doubly pleasant because the men, to express their gratitude, brought tufts of grass, something that resembled hay, and hard black biscuits which he crunched with relish between his teeth. The least interesting feature of the occasion was when the master thrust a dull, hard object under his nose and made a speech.

'Jumper,' the master said, 'you are a hero. How I wish you could understand! It was your marvellous instinct that saved us all—sensing the enemy, and disobeying even me, when I wanted to force you to ford the stream. By disobeying, you warned us of the danger, of which we were not aware. Had you been as stupid as the other horses, and as we all were, we would have been caught in a trap, taken prisoners, or killed. Do you know what I am saying? In any case, here in this notebook I have given you full credit for your wisdom, as well as our thanks. I'm sorry about the wound in your shoulder, but the doctor will soon fix that.'

Whereupon a little man whose eyes sparkled behind glasses stepped forward and gave him several uncomfortable moments. Jumper would have resisted, but the master stood by, patting and reassuring him. When the wound had been washed and covered with an evil-smelling ointment, he felt better, except for an occasional itching, and in a few days the mishap was forgotten.

But it had served to strengthen Jumper's faith in men, and his conviction that friendship with human beings lessened the hazards of life.

When he sought to communicate something of this to the chestnut as they stood below the cliff in the dusk, his friend only turned his head, and stared with hungry, tortured eyes. Jumper ran his muzzle lightly, playfully, over the chestnut's flank, as if to say, 'Cheer up, brother. You get gloomier every day. What's the matter?'

'You ask me that!' the other's hollow eyes answered. 'You incurable optimist! Can't you see that I am hardly able to drag my legs from exhaustion? It's a miracle that I am still alive. Gloomier! And why not? What is there to neigh about? Mark me, my friend, we'll never come out of this hell alive.'

The chestnut's depression was contagious, especially as Jumper too, was aware of something ominous in the air. The character of the fighting in the past few days had undergone a change. The enemy fire was continuous; while their own guns answered only now and then. Out of loyalty to each other, he and the master put on a brave show. But this self-deception, although it afforded a degree of relief, could not do away with the sense of danger and the threat of parting.

When the lieutenant came to Jumper that night his whole appearance was one of profound dejection. 'We're in a bad fix, old fellow,' he said in a sad voice. 'The enemy is surrounding us. All we can do is fight, and look forward to almost certain death or imprisonment.'

Jumper regarded the man with compassion and love, but there was also firmness in his eyes. He would not give up so easily. The instincts to live was strong in him, and he could not conceive any danger so great that it would separate him from the master, from the chestnut gelding, or even from the horrors and hardships that were his daily companions. Life could be unspeakably bad but it was preferable to death.

Chapter 27

The night of the retreat was raw, windy, and cold. The forest shadows revealed the dim shapes of men, horses, and carts, as the battery hurried from its exposed position. In the darkness the grotesque caravan stumbled forward, halted, and then stumbled forward again. There was the sound of whispered curses, as the soldiers tried to restore some semblance of order. Not infrequently they had to lend their strength to help the hungry and exhausted horses up the steep hills. Behind remained broken carts and the remains of men and horses, and the air was hideous with the cries of the wounded, whom the living were powerless to aid.

Jumper, as always when the master was riding him, for the time being forgot hunger and weariness and moved resolutely as directed—now towards the head of the retreating column, now towards its end. He was infected with the common excitement. The movement, shouts, and oaths seemed to promise release from all the recent misery. And indeed, before dawn was upon them, the entire division had reached a broad plateau sown with sharp rocks and bearing a crest of enormous cedars, larches, and pines.

Welcoming an opportunity to catch their breath after the tiring all-night march, men and horses threw themselves on the ground as if nothing else mattered. Jumper, however, still under saddle, stood tied to the wheel of a gun-carriage in the company of three other horses, among which was the chestnut gelding. He made an effort to catch the eye of the master, who was standing nearby, but without success. He slid his nose over the steel of the gun and over the ground, and withdrew it in disgust—there was nothing anywhere to appease his hunger and thirst. Several times he lifted his head, opened his mouth and distended his nostrils to inhale the early-morning wind, as if the mountain freshness had the power to dull his appetite. Once—twice—three times he struck the ground with his hoof to attract the chestnut's attention, but the gelding only raised his head to gaze listlessly for a moment at his impetuous comrade. There was something unfamiliar and terrifying about his dimmed glance and the emaciated body blackened by sweat and dust.

The world was in a sorry way! To be hungry and thirsty, neglected by the master and ignored by his old friend whom he longed to console!

When at last the master came to him, it was not to bring cheer or comfort. For a moment he stroked Jumper's sweaty shoulder, then on an impulse threw both arms around his neck and began to speak in a tender, muffled voice. Jumper stood still, trying to catch the slightest change of inflection.

'I know, my faithful Jumper, that you are hungry and thirsty, but there is nothing here but rocks. We have to stay on this hill until evening, and until reinforcements reach us. Then, if we survive, there will be time for rest and an abundance of everything. I promise you. Who knows, we may even see the mistress. You haven't forgotten her? She sends you greetings in every letter and begs God that we return to her alive and unhurt!'

As if in answer, Jumper pricked up his ears and nudged the master gently. His wise eyes seemed to say: 'Your words are meaningless to me, but believe me I understand your anxiety. Have no fear for me. It is true, I am hungry and thirsty, but so is everyone else. We'll endure it together. Only don't leave me alone. I can bear anything but that.'

Just then the master was interrupted by someone inquiring for him. Watching him go away, Jumper felt something akin to panic. A shudder ran over his body, his legs stiffened, and his head came to attention with ears cocked. In a moment his staring eyes picked out another figure approaching through the pale dawn. Snorting in fear, he tugged desperately at the rope that held him, when suddenly he recognized his friend, the bearded soldier. 'Jumper!' the man greeted him in a soothing voice. 'Why are you frightened? Didn't you recognize me? Or did the fog frighten you? Shame on you! You, an old veteran, and a mere trifle scares you. You stupid! But maybe you see something concealed from us sinful mortals. Do you? Our death, perhaps?'

Jumper was not listening. His ears, so acutely sensitive, had caught the dreadful whine of a shell, and he swung about, every nerve tense. For a moment man and horse were one in their realization that with the daylight the horror would begin again, and the heavens would rain fire and destruction.

Obediently he followed the soldier to a spot where other horses were gathered under the shelter of a projecting cliff. The next few hours were a nightmare, with shells exploding all around them, and sparks lighting the air like stars. Even the earth heaved under the terrified animals who hugged the cliff for protection against flying fragments, as well as rocks, dust, and toppling trees.

Near Jumper were the chestnut gelding and several other comrades who had shared the privations of the campaign. Farther away was the black filly whom he had courted so long without success. She was acting like one possessed, tearing at the leather thong that held her to a tree. Beyond her stood a short, broad-chested and broad-rumped bay colt for whom Jumper had no liking, because he considered him a rival. But now no one had time for thought of love or rivalry. The common danger killed all desire save one—to escape this hell of shattering noise. Step by step the barrage came closer, until a solid curtain of fire seemed to envelop them. The cliff offered only a partial protection. Suddenly from above, following a blinding explosion, came an avalanche of stones and dirt bearing with it an enormous tree. One end of the tree struck a horse, grasping it in its branches as if in an embrace, and the two disappeared over the edge. This was the first casualty of the morning, and the horses swelled the din with frantic shrieks for freedom so they could run away and hide.

At midday, a hot sun looked down on the devastated earth. The cannon fire had almost ceased, giving way to rifle fire and to a hail of bullets that came from every direction. Under this withering fire men approached, untied the horses, and led them from their temporary shelter to a place in the open where desolation and death were even more apparent. The horses went willingly enough, pressing against the men, trusting blindly that they were being led to safety.

Jumper confidently followed his friend the bearded soldier, hesitating only now and then to cast sidelong glances at the grotesque ruins heaped all around. Carefully he picked his way among the debris, jumping over shell holes, and avoiding with distaste the bodies of dead and wounded men who aroused in him endless unnamed fears. But when, a few minutes later, the lieutenant approached, tightened the saddle, and jumped on his back, all fear left him. He felt sound, safe, and strong again, and for the rest of the afternoon he gave himself up to the will of his master. From one end of the plateau to the other they travelled, and

Jumper heard with pleasure the man's loud, commanding voice, and watched horses and the lumbering equipment move at his direction towards a steep incline. Somehow the horse seemed to know that in this crisis everyone's security depended on him and on the man he was carrying.

As the afternoon progressed, the danger increased. The unseen enemy, watching their descent from the plateau, let loose a fresh rain of death. Jumper saw his rival, the bay colt, stumble and fall with his rider. Jumper quivered with excitement, but he never for an instant gave way to panic. Responding to the slightest move the master made, he went here and there, forward and back, wherever they were needed. In the midst of death he felt at one, not only with the master, but with all the struggling, roaring, screaming mass of men and horses. The only time he became frightened was when he came across the handsome filly lying in a pool of blood, her head with its staring eyes severed from the body. He would have shied away, but a light movement of the master's hand restored his calm, and he rushed to join the others pouring into a ravine where a road led to the safety of a dense forest.

At a turn near the foot of the hill he saw the chestnut gelding beside a shattered cannon. The gelding, terribly wounded, was struggling to rise, but only his forelegs obeyed. Supporting himself in a sitting position, and tossing his head helplessly from side to side, he seemed unable to understand what had happened to him. Jumper would have gone to him, but the master spurred him on, and the last chance to aid and comfort his old companion was gone forever.

Surrendering completely to the master's will, Jumper went forward. He saw the head of the column disappear from view in the forest, then another section, and still another. He heard the roar of friendly guns renewing the battle overhead. Reinforcements were at hand, and the danger past, as witnessed by the triumphant cries on every side.

But with victory in sight, Jumper's instinct failed him: he obeyed the master when he should have refused. For the last time the master turned around, and made him go towards the end of the slowly moving column. What followed was like a bolt out of the blue. Possibly it was a chance enemy shell that exploded not far from them. All Jumper knew was that the earth wavered under him, and something tossed him high into the air.

When he came to he jumped up quickly, aware of a sudden weakness in the legs, and a burning sensation that reminded him of the branding iron. The master was lying a few steps away, groaning and trying to rise. On an impulse Jumper raised his head and neighed, and soon men came on the run, among them the bearded soldier.

Standing there quietly, with warm blood trickling down his right quarter, Jumper waited for the master to get in the saddle, but instead men lifted him on a stretcher, and carried him away. Jumper stumbled after them, knowing only that his place was at the master's side. He did not hear the master's orders to the bearded soldier, instructing him that Jumper be taken to a doctor and every effort made to save his life.

Somewhere far away the artillery was still rumbling, but it was peaceful in the forest. The men carrying the wounded officer moved silently and swiftly towards their destination, and Jumper, leaving a thin trail of blood behind him, tried his best to keep up with them.

Chapter 28

The first snow of that winter found Jumper in surroundings that were entirely to his liking. He did not know how it had happened, or who was his guardian-angel, but by some good turn of fortune he was back among the familiar comforts and tranquillity of a stable yard, where all he heard were the reassuring calls of other animals. The noise they made was music to his ears, and the scent of good hay and steaming manure was like precious perfume. The people were no less comforting—gentle, solicitous of his well-being, and bearing no resemblance to the stiff, uniformed soldiers who had been so confusingly alike.

Jumper was a long way from the front lines. His new home was in a large village on the shore of the Volga. Scars that were covered by a layer of whitish-grey hair were his only reminder of the war. In every other way he seemed to be the same amiable horse, but a close observer would have noted in his large, dark eyes an absence of his old reckless spirit. Something in him was gone, and with it the desire for mischievous play and violent sport. Although he was content with his life, he seemed to be waiting for someone; whenever he heard the sound of human voices, he listened nervously, as if trying to distinguish among them the one voice he longed to hear.

Unfortunately, Jumper could not communicate with the human beings who cared for him. Otherwise he would have known that his master had died on the operating table. First, however, he had asked that Jumper be sent to his father who had a model homestead on the Volga. This wish was carried out with the assistance of the young mistress, the battery commander, the doctor, and the bearded soldier. An entry in the little notebook, which the battery commander had made in his own hand, recited the facts in brief:

'For loyalty to his master and the services rendered to his country, this remarkable horse deserves our most devoted care. I consider it my duty to carry out the last wish of his master, who died of wounds, and to send Jumper to his father's homestead where, I hope, he will find well-earned peace and rest. All those into whose hands this notebook will fall, know that we, who were his comrades in arms, honour the memory of Jumper, as we do that of his valiant master. May he live long and happily!'

Thus it happened that Jumper, at one stroke, became a hero, and was officially invalided to a comfortable stable yard in a remote village, where his every need was anticipated. Did he remember or grieve for his master? No one can say. But he recognized instantly the young mistress when, soon after his arrival at the new yard, she came to him, embraced his neck, and wept. 'Jumper, Jumper,' she said between sobs. 'You returned but he did not. How miserable we both are.' Jumper stood motionless because he long ago had learned to accept human grief, and because he sensed that the tears and incoherent words were addressed to him. Or, perhaps, it was merely a natural kindness which association with people had taught him.

The young mistress visited him several times, petted and talked to him, and then one day she, too, disappeared. Out in the yard for his exercise he looked for her in the usual places; he even went to the porch and pawed the ground, begging her to come out. When she did not appear, he wandered away disconsolately. As days went by, because he naturally liked and needed people, he transferred his affections to those who looked after his daily needs.

Before long he felt rich with friends, but the objects of his greatest attachment were a tall, grey-haired man, and a small woman who brought him bread and cried all the time she fed him. They were the master's parents, and between the three of them there was an understanding from the very beginning. Their first words took the horse to their hearts:

'Jumper,' they said, 'you were with our boy when he was wounded. . . . You shared his hardships and anxieties, and it was his wish that we look after you. In caring for you we are thinking of him. You are the living reminder of our only son.'

Jumper was rarely used for work. Occasionally he pulled the man and the woman in a light sleigh through the village streets, and waited for them outside the church. Ever so often the man saddled and rode him on an inspection round of the fields. To Jumper this was sheer pleasure. The pressure of legs against his flanks, the firm, friendly hand to guide him, and all around a sense of nature at peace—all this was as familiar and dear as the animal noises that filled the barnyard, and made him a part of a happy and contented whole.

Surrounded by people who had not known him as a colt, Jumper came to maturity, and there was none to mark the change in him. No longer did he plunge about and become excited over trifles, no longer did he prance and preen to attract an audience. He was constant and willing in the performance of his duties, and he conducted himself with the air of one who had considered the consequence of every action. While he enjoyed the noise and bluster of the barnyard, he at the same time treasured the privacy and seclusion which his own stall afforded him. He liked the society of others, but he was learning to find satisfaction within himself.

In short, he had grown up.

Nevertheless, when spring began to spread its warmth over the earth, and the melting snow revealed green patches on the hills overlooking the village, Jumper felt a resurgence of his old restlessness. He did not know the cause of it, but one day he was let out of the stable and there, waiting for him, was a chestnut filly tied to a post. He ran towards her with all his former speed and eagerness.

After that there were other fillies as the neighbouring peasants brought their mares to be bred. As suddenly as it had appeared the restlessness was gone, and Jumper entered on a life for which Nature had intended him. He was doing his share, and providing fine, healthy offspring to carry on the work for years to come.

PART IV

Chapter 29

In life nothing is constant: fine weather gives way to storms, serene, happy days are followed by dark ones, abundance by dire need. While Jumper was enjoying well-earned peace and comfort, discontent with the war and with the government was growing throughout the country. Revolution had broken out in the capital and was rolling in ever-mounting waves over every section. It reached the remote hamlets that knew nothing of the war except that it was taking away their young men.

Jumper had no share in the making of the war or of the revolution, but he could not escape the common fate. In moving from the great centres to the villages, the conflict reached out greedily, and shattered his newly found happiness.

The disaster occurred towards the end of the second winter, which Jumper had spent with his master's parents.

One morning he was waiting as usual for the day to begin, when the old man entered the stable accompanied by several men in grey coats—a uniform familiar from the war days, and one that presaged nothing good. Seizing him roughly, they led him into the yard, and with loud exclamations poked and jostled him until he was in a frenzy of excitement. It only made him more nervous when a small group of people gathered to cry and protest. When the old man and woman tried to come near him, the uniformed men pushed them unceremoniously aside. This in itself was terrifying, but he was caught wholly off guard when one of the men, driven by impatience or anger, struck him a stinging blow across the back with a leather strap. His response was immediate. He reared, lunged, and tore himself free. Then he ran, but instead of heading for the field beyond the open gate, he sought refuge in the safest place he knew—his own stall. For once his instinct deceived him. In no time the strangers were in his hiding-place. They dragged him out, beat him, and took him away. Nor did the tears of the old woman stop them.

The thing that had snatched Jumper for a second time from the life to which he was born, was an edict issued by the Soviets who had recently overthrown the Provisional Government. Horses were being drafted for the Red Army, and so it came about that Jumper found himself joining a cavalry regiment. Because of his service record described in the little black notebook he was reserved for the exclusive use of the commander of the regiment.

The commander was very impersonal. A huge, noisy, energetic man, he was always rushing from one place to another on errands that in time, he hoped, would assure him promotion to the rank of a Red Army marshal. He regarded Jumper as any other animal, simply as a convenience, and he treated him accordingly. As a result Jumper was poorly fed, seldom curried, and never petted. He lost weight, and was miserable with the civil strife raging all around him.

The regimental commander was only the first in a succession of new masters. They came and went so quickly that there was no time to form attachments. In the thick of battle Jumper felt the rider drop, and the next instant a stranger was in the saddle. It was some consolation that all around him were other horses as hungry, exhausted, and miserable as he was. At least he could count on an answer to his melancholy neighing.

He had to resign himself to the new ways of life in order to survive, but it seemed fate was merely testing him. No sooner had he accepted the idea that he could not expect anything good than another change occurred. What happened he never knew, but one night after an exchange of shots, he found himself in the care of a smooth-shaven man in a grey uniform who was somehow different from all the rest. When he spoke he made strange sounds. Even his manner of pronouncing the word Jumper seemed odd and foreign. But his voice was gentle as he thrust the familiar notebook under the horse's nose, saying:

'So you are Jumper! Well, I am glad to know you if you are such a good soldier, and such a loyal comrade. What do you say? Are you willing to serve me?'

Jumper strained his ears to catch the unfamiliar inflections of the Czech speech. Suspicious at first, he felt his uneasiness disappearing slowly. This strange man was not bad—maybe different, but not bad at all. This feeling was confirmed when the man mounted him. The way he vaulted lightly into the saddle, and exerted gentle but firm control with his knees and hands, left no room for doubt that he was a real horseman. Jumper responded happily. Here indeed was someone to respect and love. The odd speech was confusing, but the caresses and the tone of voice were much more important than words.

The Czech officer showed his interest in Jumper by personally feeding and watering him. Moreover, he curried him each morning, and permitted no one else to ride him. This suited Jumper, and to show his affection and appreciation he whinnied a low greeting every time the officer came near.

Chapter 30

Autumn was unusually warm that year. On a certain day when only peace seemed real, when aromatic, freshly harvested fields, the distant hills, and the clear skies spoke with tender regret of the summer just gone, the only discordant note in the landscape was a train hurtling eastward.

The train was a strange mixture. Immediately behind the American-made locomotive were several passenger coaches, and following them a long string of freight cars blackened by time and bearing evidence of hard use. It was a military train. The coaches were reserved for officers and soldiers of a mixed Russian-Czech cavalry regiment, and the box cars carried their mounts.

Jumper, with other horses crowded around him, was in one of the box cars. He did not know where he was going, or what was in store for him. He was without a master, although the Czech officer had been kind to him, and had provided every comfort. To move from one place to another was part of life, and he submitted to the inevitable. Certainly he had no idea that his fate was being decided in a car ahead.

It was early morning. In contrast with the monotony of the box cars, the dining-car was wild with disorder as a group of Russian and Czech officers were finishing an all-night celebration. Jackets were unbuttoned, and the untidy figures lounged around the tables covered with remnants of food and drink. Although the orderlies tried to clean out the worst of it and give the car some semblance of cleanliness in preparation for breakfast, they were unable to accomplish much. The officers were still in their cups, and not aware of their surroundings. The noise had subsided, but boastful, swaggering talk flowed as fast as ever, as each man sought to convince his neighbour of his prowess as a drinker, a lover, or a fighting adversary. Because they were cavalrymen, the conversation turned frequently to horses. A trustful listener would have been astounded by their claims, because according to their yarns their horses were supernaturally intelligent, and had a capacity for loyalty that exceeded human understanding.

A true cavalryman is like a child in his boasting. There is no limit to what he will say to prove that his favourite horse is superior to all others. And woe to the brash young sceptic who dares suggest in the presence of veteran cavalrymen that a horse lacks human intelligence. The infuriated veterans will crush him with devastating arguments and examples.

The talk went on and on, driving out of their minds the awareness of war. These man had been fighting along the Volga, and were bound for the interior of Siberia, there to reorganize and replenish their ranks. They were looking forward to a period of rest, and mixed with that anticipation was a feeling of gratefulness that their lives had been spared thus far.

Two young officers sat in a corner apart from the others, and carried on a conversation in subdued voices, without noticing the hubbub around them. One wore the uniform of a Czech captain, the other—of a Russian lieutenant. The empty bottles on the table before them showed that they had had their share of refreshments. Captain Malechek and Lieutenant Kolosov were discussing the revolution, the inevitable defeat that faced Germany since the entrance of the United States into the war, and the peace to come that promised a brotherhood of all nations. Unlike their fellow officers they had no taste for exchanging personal confidences; instead they were intent on remaking the world.

The Czech was a muscular man of imposing build, with a smooth-shaven face, and darting blue eyes. He spoke Russian with that pleasant soft accent which all educated Czechs bring to any foreign language. By contrast the Russian lieutenant had a Mongolian cast of features with prominent cheekbones and a trim, black moustache. His round face and his expressive brown eyes reflected all his emotions. The lieutenant was an impulsive man who expressed his views simply, briefly, and with self-assurance. At the moment he was calm because he and his companion were in complete agreement. During a lull in their conversation, they listened to a beefy fellow nearby who was extolling the virtues of his horse.

When the man had finished, Captain Malechek said: 'You know, although the cavalrymen are drunk and much of what they say is nonsense, I still can understand how they feel. I am a cavalryman myself. I have grown up with horses and served with them through the World War and now through the civil war. I could tell you of some remarkable experiences. I'm not saying a horse has a mind like a human being, but it has an instinctive understanding that is amazing, and a sense of loyalty that would do credit to anyone. Do you agree with me? If the subject interests you and you are not too tired, there's something I'd like to show you—the record of a horse which seems to me quite unusual.'

The lieutenant urged him on: 'By all means. I'd like to see it. Maybe we are both romantics but I feel as you do. Horses and dogs have something in their eyes that approaches human thought.'

The captain left the car, and was gone for several minutes. When he returned he carried a greasy, stained notebook which he handed to the lieutenant.

'Here it is,' he said. 'It was written by soldiers and officers unknown to me, and it is the service record of a Siberian horse, named Jumper, who was drafted during the first year of the war. He took part in a number of engagements and was wounded twice before he got to me. You'll see him—he's aboard this train. Nothing much to look at, but graceful and, as you say, there's something in his eyes. Perhaps the most unusual thing about him is that all these people—privates and officers alike—took the trouble to write about him as if he were a reasoning being and a trusted friend.'

The lieutenant opened the notebook and smiled at the title: '*Life and Service Record of the Siberian Colt Jumper*.' Opening it at random, he began to read:

'We are on the eve of defeat. We are almost surrounded. After a successful retreat our present position is more secure than our last one—which the enemy knew and shelled at random—but from here also there is no escape. We have lost more than half of our men, horses, and equipment. The supply of shells is low, and by tomorrow, unless the promised reinforcements reach us, we shall perish. There is no alternative, except to sell our lives as dearly as we can. We are worn out. Night brings but little rest. I am writing by the light of a small electric torch, under the cover of a gun-carriage—for what reason I don't know, except that I feel the need to record my gloomy forebodings. I am writing in the notebook that belongs to my faithful friend, Jumper. Perhaps we shall both die tomorrow, or one of us may survive. I cannot guess. God's will be done. But if I should be the one to die, I beg that word be sent to my beloved wife, and to my dear mother and father, asking them to take care of Jumper. It is my last wish—that he be provided with all the comforts he requires for the rest of his life. In the event Jumper survives me and falls into the hands of strangers I ask that this notebook go with him. I want people to know about his fine qualities, his loyalty, and his unusual understanding. This horse is happy when his master is happy, and unhappy when his master is sad. On many occasions I have observed how his moods reflect mine. If I am uneasy for any reason, he is nervous and restless. Tonight, for instance, I do not doubt that he is aware how deeply discouraged I am, and how lonely. He is here beside me of his own will—nothing holds him—and his wise eyes follow every move I make. I swear that they are human, and not the eyes of an animal. I should not be surprised to hear him say: "Have courage, master. I am with you, I will not leave you. Whatever comes we will share together unto death." Believe me, I have not lost my mind when I write this. The things I say about Jumper are true, remarkable as they may seem. He is a soldier by an accident of fate, and he is a good one. More than once I have known him to scent danger when there were no apparent signs of it. He is a favourite with the men of our battery, and his fame has spread to other units. It is said no other horse can match him in intelligence, or in obedience. As for me, I consider Jumper my friend, as dear to me as any soldier in my battery. It hurts me more than I can say to see him so thin, dirty, and weary. Yet if it were possible to drive him to a safe place, I know he would not leave me. He would only go a short way, and look back at me with pained amazement, as if to say: "You wish to be alone with your thoughts. Very well, I will not disturb you. But you need only call me, and I will return."

'Before a battle, every soldier feels the invisible breath of danger, and his thoughts turn not only to those dear to him who are far away, but to those close by who will share his fate. The imminence of death makes all men equal. I, too, am thinking of my loved ones and of those who tomorrow will share my fate. I find myself wondering about every human shadow that passes in the dark: will he be one of tomorrow's victims? It is not strange, then, that I think also of my fine, loyal Jumper, who trusts me so blindly. You who may be Jumper's master after tonight, remember that he has shared my personal hardships as well as the common hardships of military life. It is no sacrilege to say that he, like all of us, is in the keeping of Divine Providence. Treat him with the consideration you would show another human being. If you doubt what I have written of his wisdom, you have only to go to him, pat him, and say: "Jumper, you are a gentle horse. Serve me as faithfully and honestly, as you have served all the others who loved you and cared for you." Say that to him and I am certain he will give you proof that he understands. You also will have the satisfaction of knowing that your kindness to him is the greatest service you can render me. LIEUTENANT RADOV.'

Lieutenant Kolosov was deeply moved by the strange entry, hastily scribbled in pencil. Impulsively he said to Captain Malechek: 'This man deserves to have his last wish carried out. What do you propose to do with the horse?'

The captain shook his head. 'I don't know. My regiment got him from the enemy, and now he seems to belong to me. But I have my own horse, who has been with me from the day my squadron joined the Russian army. According to the regulations, I have no right to have two horses, and I will be forced to transfer Jumper to the commissary department when we reach our destination. I hate to do it. It is not pleasant to give him into strange hands. Unless . . .' The captain paused—struck by a sudden thought, and leaning forward, whispered: 'You love horses, you are a romantic, and have a taste for literature—you take this horse and the notebook! It is fitting that you two Siberians should be together. If you agree, consider the matter closed—we'll seal the bargain in Cheliabinsk.'

The two men rose and solemnly shook hands. They were delighted with their bargain—they felt that they were carrying out the last wish of a dead comrade, and this gave them a sense of great satisfaction.

The locomotive whistled, the sun rose higher, and in the freight car ahead Jumper stood, not knowing that his fate was being decided.

Chapter 31

People and animals are blessed alike in not knowing what the future holds, but there is one difference. People can wonder, speculate, day-dream, and plan a life exactly to their liking. Animals cannot.

Jumper accepted each day as it came. Nature that had created him looked after him, with the assistance of men. Standing in the box car, he was untroubled by memories of the past or by doubts of the future. He had not forgotten everything. Whenever he heard a sharp noise that resembled a shot he cocked his ears, and stretched his neck to its full length. And it made him nervous to have his eyes covered—it reminded him of the painful operation when a doctor had probed for the bullet that had wounded him.

There were other ways in which Jumper had changed. The most pronounced change of all was his attitude towards people, whom he had learned to divide in two groups—masters and all others. Masters were very rare and commanded his entire devotion, others were legion and a matter of indifference. For instance, the man who talked so strangely: Jumper obeyed him willingly, recognizing him as an experienced horseman and a person of kindness and good will, but he was not a master.

For the time being life was not unbearable, though it was very dull. Now and then the doors of the car rolled open, and he caught a tantalizing glimpse of fields, woods, and open sky that set his body quivering and his legs dancing. Or the sight of a filly made his blood race, and he protested against his confinement by dashing about and neighing loudly. The company of other horses offered little comfort—they were all casual acquaintances, who came and went with greater frequency than men, and unfortunate experience had taught him not to trust any of them in the matter of food and drink.

Days dragged on until one evening when the train stopped, and rough-speaking soldiers in grey led Jumper out of the car to a flimsy shelter, near a wooden trough. There he stood alone all night, watching lights come and go around the station, as shrieking locomotives with black cars swaying behind them switched back and forth. Lightning flashed, it thundered, and a sprinkling rain changed to a downpour. He neighed, but no one heard him above the storm, and there were no horses near enough to answer. An overhanging roof offered some protection against the deluge but the wind and the dampness were thoroughly unpleasant. Finding some coarse tasteless reeds in the trough, he munched them for want of something better, and waited for morning.

The station was Cheliabinsk. Here the Russian lieutenant Kolosov was to take possession of Jumper, and from here they were to continue together to the city of Ekaterinburg where the main forces of the Siberian army were concentrated.

The grey dawn found Jumper anxious and restless. He looked around suspiciously at the brown station buildings and held his ears alert for the sound of other horses, but he heard nothing to reassure him, only occasional human voices. He was utterly dejected when at long last he heard the firm tread of feet, and the clanking of spurs and swords. Lifting his head, he eyed the approaching men hopefully. They were coming in his direction—strangers all, and therefore not to be trusted. Nevertheless, he tugged at his halter, grateful for any break in the monotony.

One man in a great-coat detached himself from the group, and came straight towards him. Patting him on the neck, he said tenderly: 'Jumper, you are a fine horse. I know that you will serve me faithfully and loyally, as you have served all who loved and cared for you.'

The kindly voice and familiar Russian accent delighted Jumper, and he lunged towards the man with a whinny acknowledging the greeting. The way in which the man stroked him and felt his muscles indicated that he was a friend. Readily Jumper followed him into a box car where a couple of soldiers were busy clearing a place for him next to four other horses. There was water in the car, and mangers filled with hay, but Jumper was not interested in these luxuries. He was intent only on the man who had befriended him.

When the soldiers finished their work, and made ready to leave, Jumper let out a piercing neigh, pleading with the man to stay. In reply he heard: 'Don't worry, Jumper. I will be back.'

This seemed to satisfy him. Greedily he began to eat the hay, in his excitement throwing whole bunches of it on the floor. He was gay and contented with this new turn of fortune—not only was the hay excellent, but once again he had found a real master.

Chapter 32

Again Jumper's life returned to the ways that resembled his first happy, untroubled years. He had a master to whom he was deeply attached, and a mistress who patted and indulged him in all the little things he liked. Never had he been better cared for. Every morning a young soldier, who carried with him the familiar odour of tobacco and peasant sweat, led him out of his warm stable to be watered, groomed and fed abundantly with golden, fragant oats. And all the while he tended him the soldier talked or sang in a gay, lusty voice. Jumper could feel his flanks filling out, and his coat getting silky. The sheer joy of living made him move prankishly, every step a dance step.

His duties also were to his liking.

When he had finished his oats—he ate them without lingering—the day's work began. To Jumper it was not work but a round of activities that he enjoyed thoroughly. First, the soldiers saddled him, and having done so he tossed the reins over the saddle-bow, giving Jumper his freedom. Then came the period of the day Jumper liked best of all. Slowly, throwing out his legs with conscious grace, he ran to the porch to wait for the master. If the master was late he would paw impatiently and whinny. Usually he had not long to wait before the master appeared accompanied by the mistress.

'Good morning, Jumper,' they would greet him. 'Did you sleep well? Had your breakfast? Time for us to be off.'

This was Jumper's cue to toss his head, and to demand from the mistress his usual tribute of sugar and bread.

Before the master vaulted into the saddle, he and the mistress strolled arm-in-arm about the yard, seemingly loath to part, while Jumper walked behind them. Every so often he thrust his muzzle in their backs to remind them of his presence, or pushed his head between them as if to take part in the conversation. Occasionally, on a sudden impulse, he would toss his head in the air, shake his mane, twist his tail, and set off to circle the yard in easy, graceful strides.

He no longer dashed in wild leaps that proclaimed an exuberant, untamed spirit. Instead, he purposefully moved his powerful body out of a desire to please and to show off before the mistress, as well as to limber up his muscles.

Having completed the circle, he went to the far corner of the yard, and stood with head poised high and ears cocked—waiting. Then when he heard the master call—'Hey, Jumper, enough fooling. Time for us to go. Say good-bye to the mistress. Quick!'—he responded as if someone had pressed a button. Abandoning his coy manner, he ran, nostrils distended, with all speed back to his friends.

Jumper's attachment to the master was based on kindness, consideration, and good horsemanship. The lieutenant respected horses. When he jumped into the saddle he did not tug at the reins until the bit cut the mouth, nor did he use his crop, or worry the animal with spurs. He held the reins lightly and guided his mount with a gentle pressure of the legs, at the same time pulling one rein or the other to indicate the direction and the speed he desired. Even when Jumper misunderstood he did not lose his temper. There was reason for this. The master, though an experienced horseman, was trained as an infantry officer and had only recently, since the outbreak of revolution, assumed command of a cavalry squadron. He was perfectly aware that he made as many blunders as Jumper did.

It took a little time for Jumper to grasp what was wanted of him—implicit obedience to the will of the master which made possible mass movement of horses and riders who had to keep a fixed distance between them. When he had learned his new duties, he found them greatly to his liking and far more congenial than service in the artillery with its burdensome equipment and everlasting noise. It did not take him long to discover that he and the master had to set the pace for the others—whatever the master made him do, all the other horses had to do also. His sense of leadership was awakening in him. It pleased him to feel that he was helping to set in motion this great living mass, and when at the height of the excitement the squadron, urged on by a frightening roar of human voices, swept over a snow-covered field, he was so carried away that he had a wild desire to rush on and on . . .

The whole of that winter and early spring was spent in drills and manoeuvres. But eventually came another change, and for the worse. Again Jumper was loaded with other horses into cars, and the cars joggled towards an unnamed destination. This time, however, one circumstance lessened the tedium of the journey. Whenever the train stopped, the master came to Jumper's car and talked to him.

'The happy days are over, my friend. We are again in the war, and it is not a good war with brother fighting brother. Who knows when it will end? Happily, much of it is beyond your understanding, Jumper, or you would be as sad as I am. We're in a bad plight. But at least we had a fine winter, didn't we—you, the mistress and I?'

Jumper pawed the floor with his hoof, content to hear the master's voice, to feel his caresses, and to share his concern. With the master near him and with the same gay young soldier to wait on him, life was still good. But he was overjoyed when at last the train stopped, the horses were unloaded, and he felt the firm earth once more beneath his hoofs.

Then began an exhausting march that lasted for many days and nights. With Jumper and the master at its head, the long column of cavalry wound like a ribbon along the road, and on both sides woods and fresh fields beckoned to them. Overnight the detachment stopped in small villages where hay was abundant but there were no oats, or else they camped in a sheltered spot, near a spring, where they could feast on thick, juicy grass. But although Jumper, in common with all the horses, loved the young, green grass, when filled to repletion he was invariably uncomfortable—his stomach swelled, he felt puffy and perspired easily.

Gradually danger was added to the difficulties of the march. As the most experienced veteran among the horses, Jumper was the first to sense it.

Frequently the master took several mounted men, and rode far ahead of the detachment on excursions that had about them an air of mystery. A certain tenseness of the rein, and the silence, conveyed to Jumper the need for caution. Even in the woods the horses remained saddled, and because no fires were built they suffered from mosquitoes and from a multitude of troublesome gnats which crawled into their nostrils, and tickled their sensitive skin. Jumper switched his tail, and stamped his hoofs, but nothing helped. The gnats feared only smoke, and there was none. Motion and strong winds brought the only relief.

On these excursions they travelled most of the time through the woods, along unfrequented paths, stopping often to wait and listen. Listen for what? Jumper did not know. But this cautious progress through the woods faintly reminded him of something in his past, something associated with the Siberian taiga.

Jumper did not shy, like the other horses, when frightened partridges fluttered from under their hoofs, or when small animals scampered across their path, or when squirrels played tag just above their heads. All this was familiar to him. But his instinct warned him that the peace of the woods was deceptive.

During this march Jumper became more than ever attached to his new master; a great intimacy grew between them as the days went by, and they came to depend more and more on each other. Jumper felt that he and the master were almost one; he recognized him at a distance by his footsteps and voice, and in the darkness by his whisper, his touch, and the scent of his body. He followed the lieutenant, never letting him out of sight, and the only things that ever diverted his attention were the fillies. They were a severe provocation, and the master had frequent occasions to rebuke him, but the troopers only laughed about it.

'You, Jumper, never miss anything,' they chided him. 'A soldier cannot be caught napping when a female comes his way.'

Jumper felt encouraged by the incomprehensible words, twisted and turned with impatience, tossed his head, pawed the ground, and neighed softly.

Only weariness and a growing awareness of danger helped him to control his desire. The master spent more and more time on the mysterious forays. Often he dismounted and left Jumper behind while he and some of the men went on foot into the woods. These absences made Jumper uneasy: at every rustle he raised his head, cocked his ears, and peered anxiously at the opening where the master had disappeared. When the master returned Jumper's gentle whinny conveyed a mixture of joy and reproach. 'Why can't I go with you?' he seemed to say. 'You must know that I am anxious about you.'

The master understood and consoled him: 'You are a wise and loyal friend, but even you do not understand how necessary it is for us to take these precautions. Our enemies are watching us closely, and we must be ready. Sometimes we must crawl on our bellies, and we dare not make a sound. How can I take you along? Danger is very close, it is everywhere around us. Just wait

—your turn will come.'

His forebodings were soon justified. One day at dawn, just as the detachment emerged from a forest and started to cross a meadow, a volley of shot greeted them from a thicket. So unexpected was the attack that some of the horses forgot their training and plunged back into the woods, paying no heed to their riders. Their instinct was stronger than their training. The detachment was forced to retreat, and Jumper went last, without hurry, giving the master time to observe the exact position of the enemy. As soon as they disappeared among the trees, the firing stopped, but they had been discovered, and trouble was ahead.

The master was jubilant with pride. As he tightened the saddle straps, he talked to Jumper affectionately: 'You're a great fellow. It's easy to see that you are a veteran, and not afraid of bullets. Now's the time, brother, for you to show your mettle. Our chances depend on your strong legs and your endurance.'

Jumper tossed his head with excitement and delight. He knew that he was being praised. His confident attitude said: 'Trust me, master. I've been through this before, and much worse. Get on and I'll carry you to safety.'

As the day went on the danger became more apparent. Whenever the detachment was in the open it was instantly fired on, but they had accomplished something useful. Their duty was to reconnoitre and they had discovered a considerable enemy force. The enemy's purpose was to keep the master's troops in sight until reinforcements arrived so they could encircle them. The only sensible thing to do was to retreat and hide in the hills. . . .

The detachment moved chiefly at night, led by a guide dressed as a peasant. The country was real Siberian taiga—tall, slender pines and larches covering rolling hills and cliffs concealed by moss. The troops moved in single file, following the thread of a footpath that was broken by tumbling streams. Jumper stepped cautiously, remembering the lessons of long ago. His instinct told him to avoid the sharp stones hidden in the grass, and the smooth slippery rocks that formed the beds of streams. Something told him: 'Save these legs at all cost, for upon them everything depends.'

Behind him the other horses moved awkwardly, slipping and catching themselves as their riders grumbled and cursed. Ahead of him rode the guide mounted on a strong stocky chestnut who reminded Jumper of his old friend. He tried to get close and strike up a friendship, but the other was wary and kept his distance. His confident bearing showed him as a true son of the taiga, and Jumper soon discovered that it was safest to imitate his movements.

The road became more difficult as it led sharply up the face of a cliff, and then down into a gorge. During the day they halted, and lay hidden in a thicket. The horses were never unsaddled, no fires were built, and the men spoke in unnaturally subdued voices and were not allowed to smoke. Once the enemy almost overtook them, and there was a fierce exchange of shots. Darkness was the only thing that saved them, and made possible their escape through a ravine.

Jumper was confused about the nature of the danger. In his former war experience he had been able to distinguish the enemy by their voices and their unfamiliar scent, but now there seemed to be no difference between friend and foe. He could not possibly know that now he was engaged in a civil war, with Russians pitted against Russians, but he understood that the danger was real. Two horses that had fallen dead at his side and the groans of wounded men confirmed his fears, and at night, when the silence was intense, he kept alert for any noise that betrayed a strange presence. He knew the sounds the wind made, the rustle of small forest animals, and the night cry of owls, but anything else brought him instantly to attention and set him to pawing the ground.

The master trusted Jumper's instinct and always came to him at the first sign of restlessness. 'Yes, Jumper,' he would say, stroking him, 'you are right. There is danger. We are being pursued. Although our guide is one of the best, the enemy also has someone who knows these woods and hills.'

Jumper felt reassured, and looked as if he were saying: 'Don't misunderstand me. I'm afraid of nothing. We'll get away. You can depend upon me.' It was like a horrible game of hide-and-seek. The hills and woods looking on might well have asked themselves: 'What are these strangers doing here? What do they hope to achieve with all this horror?'

The detachment had lost several men and horses, and others were wounded. Jumper accepted the losses as a part of the fortunes of war until a particularly sharp engagement after which he looked in vain for the chestnut who always led the way. He was replaced by a clumsy, heavy grey gelding with thick shaggy legs and a short tail. The stupid creature shied at every shot, and the guide had a difficult time with him. His movements were so erratic that Jumper no longer tried to follow him, and carefully picked his own way across streams and fallen trees.

The soldiers marvelled at Jumper's instinct. Seeing him halt, raise his head, and cock his ears, they would rein in their horses and say quietly to one another: 'Look, Jumper has stopped. He senses something. Better watch out! That horse knows plenty!'

They also marvelled at the commander, who never tied Jumper when they stopped to rest, and never bothered to pull him along by the bridle when he walked. Jumper stood wherever the master left him, or followed obeying the master's commands.

These qualities won the hearts of the soldiers, and they showered Jumper with attentions. Plain, superstitious fellows, they came to regard him as a mascot, and to believe that as long as Jumper was with them they would succeed in their undertaking.

There came a day when the position of the troop appeared hopeless. The enemy was closing in. As a last resort, Jumper and eight other horses were chosen to take part in a delaying action that might give the others a chance to escape.

Under the cover of a fog, the rest of the troops moved farther into the hills. Jumper watched them uneasily, but he found comfort in the knowledge that the master stayed with him. He betrayed no excitement when with the other horses he was led to a spot sheltered by a cliff, and tied to a tree while the men took up a position on the hill.

When dawn broke the enemy opened fire. Bullets whizzed overhead, and burrowed into the earth as they struck the hill without causing damage. Jumper stood motionless, gazing at the master, ready to rejoin him at the first signal. His calmness affected the other horses; they shuddered at the sound of gunfire, but, like Jumper, they did not plunge and stood watching the men.

For two days and nights they held their ground and at every opportunity launched a counter-attack that drew the enemy away from the retreating detachment. In this dangerous game everything depended upon the endurance of the horses. Because of his coolness under fire Jumper was invariably used in the most hazardous operations.

The diversion proved successful, though it cost the lives of two men and three horses. On the third day the enemy withdrew and the firing ceased. The horses rejoiced to be rid of their saddles, to feast on a patch of succulent grass, and to hear the men's gay laughter as they sat around a fire.

Two days later with loud shouts and cheers the rear-guard joined the rest of the troop. Not long afterwards the detachment entered a village where the main force was waiting.

Everyone was in a jubilant mood. Jumper was pleased to have the soldiers gather around and admire him.

'Look at Jumper,' they said. 'He is braver and wiser than any man. A real hero!'

'Hee-ee-aa!' Jumper replied triumphantly. It was indeed a splendid world.

Chapter 33

Not knowing the causes for his misfortunes, and innocent of any wrong, Jumper found the civil war most trying. Rain or snow, heat or frost, he performed his duties without a chance to rest. He was always tired, often hungry, and only on rare occasions knew the luxury of a warm stable.

Sickness followed misery as he developed a cough accompanied by a complete lassitude that left him indifferent even to food and the affectionate ministrations of those who attended him. When the master came to see him he whinnied plaintively, begging to be helped.

'The poor beast looks at you like a sick child,' the soldier said, and then tried to cheer Jumper: 'Keep your chin up. The master will make you well.'

And the master did come to the rescue. At first Jumper protested violently when his head was pulled back and pinned against the cross beam as an evil-tasting liquid was forced down his throat. But when his cough subsided and his appetite returned, he somehow associated his improved condition with the vile medicine, and he ceased to struggle against it. He submitted willingly to the master when he rubbed his chest and legs with a smelly mixture before wrapping him in warm blankets.

The master clearly was a man of knowledge and understanding. Jumper followed his every movement with grateful eyes, uneasy whenever he was out of sight for any length of time. Then the thing he feared most happened. For two long, unhappy days he did not see the master. On the third morning the soldier with some strangers entered the stable and led him away, though he neighed and struggled desperately. They took him through a cold blinding snow to the railway line, and when he tried to break away forced him with cries and blows into a car where other frightened horses were waiting.

The dreary journey that followed was a repetition of his earlier experiences. Nervous, ever on the alert for the sound of the opening door that might bring the master, he gradually lapsed into indifference as time brought nothing but disappointment.

Long ago he had been taken west to fight in the war; now, over the same road, he was returning east to Irkutsk. Unbeknown to him, chance was bringing him back to the city where he had begun his military career.

Happiness brings to men and animals a physical sensation that is like the sun in a northern spring. That is how Jumper felt when he was led out of the car into the bustling streets of a city. The day was raw and windy, but the soft snow under his hoofs was a carpet spread over the firm, solid earth. Happily he trotted behind the sleigh, feeling the kinks leaving his body with every step.

The journey across the city eventually brought him to a large stable full of fragrant straw and hay. The stable was warm and comfortable, but after being with the other horses in the box car, he found it lonely. He paced about, uncertain what to think of this sudden turn of fortune. Soon his suspicions subsided, and he enjoyed having room to move without running into obstructions. Jumper felt curiosity stirring in him. He went from corner to corner, thrusting his nose deep into the straw and scattering it with a quick toss of the head, stopping occasionally to paw the hard, wooden floor. Finally, when he tired of this, he went to a small open window, raised his head and neighed. There was no sadness or joy in his call, only a query:

'Where am I? Why does no one come to see me?'

In answer he heard human voices and hasty footsteps approaching the stable. The sounds excited him, and he began to spin round and round like a top. When the door opened he stopped dead in his tracks as a shudder ran over his body, and his eyes strained in the semi-darkness to recognize the familiar figure of the master—the master whom he believed he had lost. With a joyous snort he rushed forward.

What a wonderful morning that was! With the master was the mistress, whom Jumper had almost forgotten. As excited as he was, they petted him and said:

'Hello, Jumper! Hello, darling! Don't be angry with us because you had to travel alone. We were waiting for you. . . . So, you haven't forgotten us? No, we can see that you have not. But how thin you are! Never mind, we'll fix that up. . . . If only you could talk and tell us where your home is. Judging by your notebook it must be somewhere near here.'

Jumper was interested only in the caresses, for which he was starved, and in the bread and sugar dainties. He went from one to the other, taking special care not to lose a single crumb as his soft lips picked each morsel from the mistress's palm.

Later, when he felt the familiar weight of the master on his back, the firm pressure of his knees, and his sure hands on the reins, he was filled with joy. He capered and danced along the streets, throwing out his forelegs with conscious grace, and begging to be allowed to run at full speed. He no longer was tired or indifferent; instead he was anxious to please and to show his strength. This, he knew instinctively, was the life for which he was intended.

Unfortunately, after a brief interval he and the master were off to war again. Leaving his stable and the newly found comforts was all that mattered. Jumper was not concerned and did not care that the ruinous civil war was drawing to an end, that the Red and White armies were uniting against a common enemy in the Far East, the notorious Ataman Semenov and his Japanese allies, or that the master was in command of one of these newly formed detachments. He became aware of the difference only when a group of strange little men passed him, and he caught an odd, foreign odour. He snorted, not knowing that he would encounter many such bands of half-frozen Japanese prisoners.

The march eastward to Lake Baikal was made through blizzard and cold that worked extreme hardship on horses and men. The detachment advanced or retreated at the dictation of the master, stumbled through woods where the naked branches dumped their burden of wet snow, or waded across fields of belly-deep, white drifts. Horses and men went hungry and cold, and died of bullets and exhaustion. Infrequently there was relief from this madness, when firing ceased and they were a long way from the enemy. Then campfires were built and there was warmth and temporary peace.

Even when his joints were stiff with cold, Jumper devoured his meagre portion of hay, tossed on the snow. The rations were so small that they intensified rather than appeased hunger. Tied for hours to a tree, he gnawed at the bitter bark to warm himself and to deaden the pains in his stomach. He endured everything without complaint, like an automaton blindly obeying his master's will.

One morning when the snow was heavier than usual, and the

cold air made breathing difficult, Jumper was electrified to find ice under his hoofs. He snorted to clear his nostrils and to catch the tantalizing scent that was in the air. His eyes and ears were on the alert, and a strange eagerness possessed him.

Having arrived on Lake Baikal, the detachment was greeted by scattered artillery fire from hidden enemy positions. Few of the shells found their mark but the explosions pierced the ice, and made holes through which water spouted only to freeze instantly in sharp, uneven patterns. In places the surface of the lake was as smooth as glass, but in others it was covered with treacherous snowdrifts that made travelling hazardous. Above the shouts of soldiers, punctuated by an occasional command, could be heard a peculiar droning sound that came from somewhere below.

The farther the detachment travelled on the ice, the more nervous Jumper became, showing clearly that he found the undertaking most distasteful. In desperation the master several times had to press the spurs into his flanks and jerk the reins to urge him on.

'What is the matter with you, Jumper?' he asked at last. 'This is not the first time you have travelled on ice. What is frightening you? Surely not this scattered firing. No one can hit anything in this weather. Go ahead!'

What the master could not understand, and what Jumper could not tell him, was that this icy plain with its strange noises reminded him dimly of something he had forgotten long ago. What was it? Why did he find it so disturbing? He knew only that he was on familiar ground. When the blizzard passed, and he could see the high, wooded hills ahead, his restlessness increased. He shivered feverishly, and when finally the detachment halted, he twisted, turned, and snorted.

The master tried to soothe him but his voice was anxious: 'Jumper, I can't make you out today. I've never seen you like this before. I'm sure it isn't the danger that frightens you. Perhaps you don't recognize us when we are covered with snow and ice. Or—God forbid—you may be ill.'

Confidingly Jumper turned towards the master, slanting his eyes as if to say: 'I don't know myself what is wrong with me. Certainly it is not fear, but this crackling and droning noise beneath the ice, and this whole country are very familiar. I must have been here before, though I can't remember.'

The following day, after a march of twenty miles and fierce

encounter with the enemy, they approached the large and prosperous village of Kabansk. They advanced slowly, and cautiously, not certain of their welcome. But when after a wait the scouts returned with a group of peasants and reported that the enemy had fled in a panic, the men plunged headlong into the village, eager to find a warm place to rest.

It was late at night, but the streets teemed with excitement as the villagers—men, woman, and children—turned out to welcome the soldiers. Shouts rang out, bells sounded merrily from church steeples, doors were thrown open to the unexpected guests. Obviously the people were glad to be rid of Ataman Semenov and the Japanese.

Infected by the common excitement, Jumper grew more nervous than ever, and pranced and plunged until the master found it difficult to restrain him. In the yard of a prosperous farm where they found shelter for the first time in days a soldier unsaddled him, rubbed him dry, and installed him, snugly blanketed, in a small stable. The place was small, but it was comfortable, warm, and smelled appetizingly of fresh hay. Yet Jumper could not stand still, and he refused the hay though he had not eaten for a long time.

The master came, stroked him, and examined him carefully. 'Jumper, I simply don't recognize you,' he said. 'I am at a complete loss to know what to do for you. As far as I can see, rest is all you need, but you won't rest.'

Every minute that passed added to Jumper's unrest. That peculiar crackling of the ice on the lake . . . this village and yard . . . everything filled him with an indefinable longing. When the master went to the house, and he was alone, he turned nervously, thrusting his nose everywhere, inspecting and smelling everything. Suddenly he raised his head and listened.

Footsteps were approaching the stable, and with them a youthful voice which kept repeating: 'Jumper, Jumper.' There was a pause, and then the door opened. Jumper was tense, as he stepped back to avoid the light from the lantern which shone in his eyes.

Framed in the doorway stood a tall, bearded man, an old woman wrapped in a shawl, and a lanky boy with one leg shorter than the other.

Jumper was motionless as the three came closer, touched his ears, and by the light of the lantern examined the brand on his quarter. He no longer quivered as he watched these people with a strange interest. When the man again stroked his ears, he nuzzled him in a friendly way. Laughing and crying, the three flung themselves on him.

'Jumper, Jumper . . .' they said. 'Denis was not mistaken. It really is you—a soldier back from the war. We have mourned you for dead, and here you are alive and well. Welcome home!'

Jumper stood quietly, as though all this time he had been waiting for them to restore his calm. But when they left him, he began to pace the stable anxiously. From time to time he neighed, and was not happy until an answering neigh came from a nearby corral.

On this night of all nights he did not want to be alone.

Chapter 34

Next morning was clear and crisp. The sun shining on the snow made it sparkle like diamonds. Hills, fields, trees, houses, granaries—everything was blanketed with white. Only the corrals stood out like dark stains on the landscape.

A festive spirit was in the air. The villagers of Kabansk were excited by the rumour that Jumper had miraculously been returned to their esteemed friend and neighbour Ozerov. One by one they hastened to see and hear for themselves. From early morning they had been gathering until a great crowd of men, women, and children—looking like dolls in their winter clothes—stood in the yard discussing the amazing news. They were all in agreement that this was nothing short of a miracle.

Jumper stood tied to a post in the centre of the eager, shouting throng. He did not understand the reason for the excitement, but the joyful voices and the caressing hands on his back and neck made him happy. From time to time he glanced out of the corner of his eye at the master, or at the bearded old man, or at the woman in the shawl, or at the boy.

The last two were beside themselves. 'Our Jumper! Our soldier! Home again!' they exclaimed over and over.

Though pleased by the attention, Jumper was constantly distracted by the noises that came from the corrals. He neighed for the sake of getting an answer, and to attract the notice of a fine piebald filly in a distant enclosure who appealed to him strangely. She did not deign to respond, but she turned her head and regarded the crowd curiously.

As the daylight grew stronger, so did Jumper's familiarity with the place. He waited for something to explain the puzzle. Then, growing impatient, he summoned all his strength for a resounding neigh that carried to the hills and back. 'Hee-ee-aa.'

As if waiting for this sign, the piebald filly lifted her head and answered Jumper with a neigh as eager as his own.

In the meantime the din of voices swelled in volume and suddenly stopped as old man Ozerov addressed the master:

'Your excellency, Mr. commander, comrade commander, I swear to you that Jumper is our horse. Look at the brand on his quarter, and at the way his ears are slit. The people here will tell you that this is the Ozerov brand. And would I—an old man—be likely to lie to you? Before God I swear that he was born right in this yard, there in that little stable. . . . We cared for him as we would for a child. Then the war came. Our children were called into the army, and Jumper was drafted along with the other horses. This was in the first year of war. Now that the war is over, give him back to us. The soldiers have returned long ago. Why should he continue to suffer? I would not ask you for any other horse, but Jumper is clever, and he understands everything. I would hate to lose him again after his miraculous return!'

In his excitement old Ozerov had removed his hat and his grey head nodded and shook, keeping time with his words. In spite of the cold there was perspiration on his forehead. He found it difficult to choose the right words, but he was afraid to stop before the commander was ready to grant his request. He went on:

'Take a good look at him,' he pointed to Jumper. 'See how he struggles. Believe me, he recognizes his home, and his first love. That piebald filly over there is the mother of his son. A splendid son he was, too; resembled his father, but the accursed bandits of Ataman Semenov and the Japs stole him from us. Let me take his bridle off, and you'll see that he will go straight to her. Have pity on him. Horses love peace as much as men. . . .'

The commander was moved. He walked over to Jumper. 'All right, old man, let's try him. But even if I am convinced that Jumper belongs to you, how can I leave him here? He is my horse, we both belong to the army, and for us the war has not ended.'

As he spoke, he removed the bridle. Jumper, feeling it slip off, tossed his head, and nuzzled the master to show his gratitude before turning and making straight for the corrals. He did not go to the nearest one which held a herd of horses, instead he joined the piebald filly in the one farthest away.

The people shouted, seeing that the filly did not run but stood quietly as Jumper nosed her all over. This was proof, and all their simple minds required, that his return was the will of God. They took it for granted that the affair concerned them as much as it did Ozerov.

A voice came out of the crowd:

'Look, they recognize each other! This indeed is a miracle. It will be sinful if we cannot persuade the commander to leave Jumper here. The horse has earned a rest, and the village needs him for breeding.'

All that day the peasants milled about in noisy turmoil. Towards evening they chose a committee to help Ozerov plead with the commander. They reasoned that he might listen if the village were to promise that Jumper would have food and care until the end of his days.

They met at Ozerov's house while the old woman and the boy Denis looked on with imploring eyes. The commander listened gravely as they addressed him, bowing and repeating word for word what had already been said.

'Take pity on us, and on Jumper, and leave him with us. He has suffered enough, poor fellow, and the entire village needs him for breeding.'

Ozerov was the last one to speak:

'Before God and the holy icons I promised at Jumper's birth that if he lived I would give him as a present to my son, Denis. The Lord answered my prayer. From the day he was born Jumper was as a brother to the boy. Since the war ended Denis has been begging me: "Father, can't we look for Jumper? Maybe he is still alive and we can bring him home." To lose him again now would break the boy's heart. . . . God will be merciful to you, believe me, if you will give Jumper back to him. As for me, I will gladly give you two perfectly good horses in exchange for him.'

The commander could resist no longer. He smiled at the boy, then turned to Ozerov and winked.

'All right, old man! I have no right to discharge a perfectly good horse, but I have noticed lately that Jumper is ailing—so if you will give me a healthy horse in exchange, I will call it a deal. I hate to part with him, but a sick horse is useless in war. I am sure you understand! . . . I will prepare the papers releasing Jumper from military duties on account of health.'

Like bees, the peasants swarmed around the commander, shouting and shaking his hand, while Denis and his mother cried and laughed.

That evening the Ozerovs gave a supper to celebrate the occasion. When the table was cleared the commander was told the story of Jumper's birth, and of his life until the day he was drafted. The commander, in turn, produced the notebook, and read to them Jumper's service record. Nodding and crossing themselves, the peasants listened in amazement. 'That is a real record,' they said. 'Sounds like a fairy tale.'

When the commander finished reading Ozerov spoke solemnly:

'Animals like people are close to God. How could Jumper have returned home without His will and mercy? May God reward those who have shown him kindness and love. May God reward you, too, Commander, for what you have done. . . .' He hesitated. 'Do not think me presumptuous, if I ask you for one more favour. . . .'

The old man scratched the back of his head in obvious embarrassment. His eyes betrayed a fear that he might spoil everything by asking for too much.

'Do not be afraid,' the commander encouraged him. 'Speak out, and if it is in my power I shall gladly do it.'

Ozerov pointed at the boy. 'My son, Denis, wishes to study to be a veterinary, and he has my blessing. Fortunately God has endowed him with a love for animals, because, as you can see, his lameness makes him unfit for hard peasant labour. He also loves to study. Most of all he loves books about animals. Just now, while you were reading Jumper's notebook to us he whispered in my ear: "Father, ask the commander for the notebook." To him Jumper is a hero, and his return—a real miracle. . . . Be generous, and give the notebook to him.'

The commander beckoned to the boy. 'Take it, Denis,' he said, handing the notebook to him. 'Like Jumper, it belongs to you.'

The boy pressed the dog-eared volume to his heart. His face was beaming, as it had on that unforgettable night when Jumper was born.

The following morning the sun was high in the skies when the detachment was ready to leave. The gay voices of the cavalrymen were blending into a marching song:

> 'I'm spending my last day with you, my friends.
> At dawn tomorrow all my family will weep. . . .'

The village turned out to the last man to see the soldiers off and to wish them good luck. Jumper alone watched the proceedings with amazement and anxiety. Groomed and shining, his head held high, he stood tied to a post in the yard. He could not understand why he was not saddled.

'Good-bye, Jumper! Good-bye, old comrade,' the master whispered in his ear. 'I am sorry to leave you, but I am happy for your sake. You are home, and you are in good hands. You will be happy here!'

He stroked Jumper, patted him, then with a quick movement vaulted on another horse that was waiting, and without looking back rode out of the yard.

Jumper turned and twisted restlessly, feeling that something was wrong. But when he heard the piebald filly neigh he stood still. His answer comforted and reassured her; he seemed to be saying: 'Don't worry! I am not going away any more. Silly girl! Don't you know that I have my honourable discharge, and am no longer a soldier?'

No sooner were the soldiers out of sight than the life of the yard absorbed him completely. The old man and woman, the lame boy and his eager caresses, the ageing dog who was forever getting underfoot, the farm noises that were music to his ears—all this was a part of him, as if he had never been away.

This was his home, beloved and real.

TITLES IN THIS SERIES

DEVIL'S HILL NAN CHAUNCY
THE EAGLE OF THE NINTH ROSEMARY SUTCLIFF
EARTHQUAKE ANDREW SALKEY
THE EDGE OF THE CLOUD K. M. PEYTON
FLAMBARDS K. M. PEYTON
FLAMBARDS IN SUMMER K. M. PEYTON
FLY-BY-NIGHT K. M. PEYTON
A GRASS ROPE WILLIAM MAYNE
HURRICANE ANDREW SALKEY
IN SPITE OF ALL TERROR HESTER BURTON
THE INTRUDER JOHN ROWE TOWNSEND
JUMPER NICHOLAS KALASHNIKOFF
KNIGHT CRUSADER RONALD WELCH
THE LITTLE BOOKROOM ELEANOR FARJEON
LITTLE KATIA E. M. ALMEDINGEN
MINNOW ON THE SAY A. PHILIPPA PEARCE
NORDY BANK SHEENA PORTER
PASTURES OF THE BLUE CRANE H. F. BRINSMEAD
PIPPI GOES ABOARD ASTRID LINDGREN
PIPPI IN THE SOUTH SEAS ASTRID LINDGREN
PIPPI LONGSTOCKING ASTRID LINDGREN
PIRATE'S ISLAND JOHN ROWE TOWNSEND
RIDE A NORTHBOUND HORSE RICHARD WORMSER
A SAPPHIRE FOR SEPTEMBER H. F. BRINSMEAD
SIRGA RENÉ GUILLOT
TANGARA NAN CHAUNCY
TIGER IN THE BUSH NAN CHAUNCY
TOM'S MIDNIGHT GARDEN A. PHILIPPA PEARCE
WARRIOR SCARLET ROSEMARY SUTCLIFF
WHEN JAYS FLY TO BARBMO MARGARET BALDERSON